Boys, Sex & Media
Helping Boys Make Smart Decisions about Sex in a Popular Culture Dominated by Stereotypes & Sexism

Crystal Smith

Copyright © 2015 Crystal Smith. All Rights Reserved. No part of this publication may be reproduced, stored in a retrieval system, or transmitted, in any form or by any means, electronic, mechanical, photocopying, recording, or otherwise, except for the inclusion of brief quotations in a review, without prior permission in writing from the publisher, Crystal Smith.

Crystal Smith, Author & Publisher

ISBN 978-0-9918435-0-3

Cover Image *Silhouette of female legs* © Gera Ovchinnikov | Dreamstime.com:

For boys everywhere who need honest answers about sex, relationships, and love.

Contents

Acknowledgments i
Preface 1
Introduction 3
Chapter 1—The Implicit Meanings in Explicit Content 9
Chapter 2—Pornography: The "Elephant on the Screen" 19
Chapter 3—Swagger and Boys' Sexual Health 33
Chapter 4—No Means No, or Does It? Cultural Confusion Over Consent 53
Chapter 5— When Things Go Too Far: Sexual Aggression, Harassment, and Assault 63
Chapter 6—Size Does Matter 87
Chapter 7—What Parents Can Do To Combat Sexualized Media Messages 103
Appendix A— Further Reading 133
About the Author 147
Bibliography 149
Index 161

Acknowledgments

This book would never have come to fruition without the unconditional support of my husband, Karl Zelem. I spent many a long day and night locked away reading, writing, deleting, writing again, deleting some more, then arriving—much later than planned—at the final product. It was an arduous process made infinitely easier by his patience and understanding. Thanks, Karl, for giving me the time and space I needed to transform that giant box of journal articles into something coherent, and for being such an ace dad.

Thanks also to my sons Nikolas and Eliot. You are always foremost in my mind and the main motivation for the work I do. You inspire me constantly with your thoughtfulness, kindness, creativity, and wisdom. I know it wasn't always easy to see me so absorbed in my work, but you both showed consideration and respect beyond your years in giving me quiet time for researching and writing.

I'm very fortunate to have the support of many family members and friends. This book took considerably more effort than my first. I tossed out multiple drafts and started from scratch more than once. Thanks to everyone who listened and offered endless encouragement during the writing process: Marilyn Mackenzie, Chantal Smith, Mackenzie Smith, Brenda Coonan, Ginny Fanthome, Michelle Walsh, and Caroline Fleury.

Since the publication of my first book I have connected with an incredible network of people who work tirelessly to draw attention to the inequities in our world. Thanks to all of you for doing what you do and motivating me to keep going: Lori Day, Melissa Atkins Wardy, Michele Sinisgalli-Yulo, Marci Warhaft-Nadler, Jennifer Shewmaker, Amy Jussel, Regina Yau, Sharon Haywood, Pia Guerrero, Rebecca Hains, Erin McNeill, and Jenn Neilson.

Lastly, a huge thanks to the fans and followers of The Achilles Effect on Facebook and Twitter for sharing your thoughts and enlightening me with opinions and perspectives that differ from my own. I love your passion and determination to change the way boys are viewed and treated in our culture!

Preface

Sex is inescapable in our popular culture and media. It is visible to audiences of all ages in sitcoms, cartoons, graphic novels, video games, magazines, music videos, and in sexual (and often objectifying) imagery on billboards, storefronts, and advertisements for everything from salad dressing to wireless speakers. New vocabulary has been created to describe the increase in erotic imagery in our culture—terms like "pornification" and "porn chic" appear regularly in the news, drawing attention to the growing similarity between the X-rated and the everyday in our media, clothing shops, newsstands, and book stores.

Against this backdrop, as my older son approached the age of 13, I wanted to learn more about what he would be up against. What types of sexual messages and imagery would he encounter in our media and wider culture, and how would he interpret them? What role would his friends play in his sexual socialization? What could my husband and I do as parents to ensure he developed a healthy attitude toward sex?

In my quest for answers to those questions, I uncovered a good deal of academic research about media and cultural influences on boys' sexual socialization, but nothing that collected the various studies into a single resource for parents and caregivers. I wrote *Boys, Sex & Media* to fill that void.

I approach this book with an open mind about teens and sex. Adolescence is a time of sexual development and curiosity. Interest in sex is normal and healthy at this age. As adults, I believe we should not fault boys for seeking out sexual information nor deny them the opportunity to explore their sexuality. Rather, we should open the lines of communication, ensuring that boys have the tools they need to critique and evaluate the sexual messages around them and the wherewithal to apply only the healthy and positive lessons to their lives.

Introduction

> "Hot dammit
> Your booty like two planets
> Go head and go ham sandwich
> Whoa, I can't stand it
> 'Cause you know what to do with that big fat butt
> Wiggle, wiggle, wiggle"[1]
> Jason Derulo

It doesn't take much imagination to decipher the meaning of "ham sandwich" in the lyric from *Wiggle* cited above, but rapper Snoop Dogg offers further explanation later in the song: "Completely separated/Till I deeply penetrate it/Then I take it out and wipe it off/Eat it, ate it, love it, hate it."

Wiggle peaked at number 5 on the *Billboard* Hot 100 chart in June 2014.[2] By March of 2015, the song's video had more than 499 million views and over 1.6 million "likes" on *YouTube*. By December of the same year, the numbers had increased to more than 670 million views and some 2.3 million likes. By all standards *Wiggle* was a monster hit, despite lyrics that would give most parents fits.

For the uninitiated, the words in *Wiggle* may seem shocking but they are standard fare in a popular music landscape littered with overtly sexual language and imagery. Whether they go the direct route—as rapper 2Chainz does when he rhymes "genius" with "suck my penis" on Derulo's other top ten hit *Talk Dirty*—or take a more indirect approach with euphemistic turns of phrase like "taste my raindrops" (an allusion to oral sex, also from *Wiggle*), musical artists are not holding back when it comes to explicit descriptions of sex.

Although the coarse language many artists employ might seem edgy or radical to young listeners, it actually reflects some very dated and traditional attitudes. Primary among them are stereotypes of men as aggressive "sexual animals"[3] and women as passive sexual objects. Or, in the language of

Derulo and Snoop Dogg, women as big fat butts to be penetrated by men. The video for *Wiggle* lays out these stereotypes within its first few seconds, showing Derulo in bed with eight women before cutting to shots of more women twerking in barely-there shorts and Snoop Dogg leering at them through an oversized pair of binoculars.

Stereotyped sexual content is not limited to music, of course. It can be found in video games, magazines, advertising, and X-rated films. Variations on the theme of sex-starved males and sexed-up females also appear in the films and television programs aimed at an adolescent audience. This highly sexualized media environment creeps in on teens during a crucial period of their development; a time of "dramatic transformation" when boys and girls are trying to establish an identity of their own, independent of their parents. As psychologists Amy Slater and Marika Tiggeman note, adolescence is also a "time of increased introspection and self-consciousness" when teens become preoccupied with their image and what other people think.[4] Choices about music and other entertainment are a way for teens to telegraph their identity to others and show that they fit in with their peer group.

So what happens when the media with which teens choose to identify is blatantly sexual and sexist? That is a question that haunts many parents.

Parents of daughters can choose from an abundance of resources about the effects of sexy media on girls. The sexualization of girlhood has, justifiably, become a major topic of conversation, with multiple books being published about the subject in 2014 alone. Female sex role stereotypes, sexual objectification, and body image have also garnered headlines.

For parents of boys it is a different story. Although boys growing up in our highly sexualized media environment face many of the same issues as girls, discussions of boys' sexual development focus disproportionately on pornography and sexual aggression. This narrow scope leaves boys cast primarily as aggressive consumers of sexualized female bodies rather than people with their own questions and insecurities about sex.

This is not to say that male sexual aggression isn't a problem. While I was writing this book, stories of harassment and assault made headlines with shocking regularity. News of gang rapes in India[5] and Steubenville, Ohio[6] emerged shortly after I started writing, soon to be followed by the tragic stories of Rehtaeh Parsons[7] and Audrie Pott.[8] Both girls took their own lives after being gang raped then harassed when pictures of the crimes committed against them were circulated among their peers. Later, sexual assault allegations against CBC broadcaster Jian Ghomeshi and American comedian Bill Cosby surfaced, as did stories of online sexual harassment of female students by male members of the Faculty of Dentistry at Dalhousie University.

In *Boys, Sex & Media* I will address the male sexual aggression evident in those crimes, along with related subjects like female sexual objectification, rape myths, and confusion over consent. But I will also look at topics that are rarely considered in discussions of boys and sex— sexual health and education, male sex role stereotypes, and body image—remembering that boys are just as confused and uncertain as girls about sex, yet often left to figure things out on their own, within the pressure cooker of societal expectations about manhood and masculinity.

In our society, masculinity and sexual identity are closely linked and boys with more sexual experience are often considered more "manly." Boys who are tentative around girls or shy about their emerging sexuality can suffer in a sexualized culture that teaches them to embrace their inner Lothario and become lusty pursuers of sex. Sexual harassment affects some 40% of middle- and high-school-aged boys in the United States and about half of the cases involve a boy being called "gay" in a negative way,[9] a sign that his manhood is being called into question.

The male body is another indicator of masculinity and it is being displayed in an increasingly sexualized manner in pop culture and advertising. This emphasis on the eroticized male physique is one reason that body dissatisfaction—an affliction that has long plagued girls—is becoming more common among boys.

In a media culture where the consequences of unsafe sex are rarely discussed, sexual health is also an area of concern for boys, particularly sexually transmitted infections (STIs) which are increasing sharply among teens of both sexes.

As the examples above demonstrate, there is real potential in our sexualized media environment for negative impacts on boys. Indeed, research has shown that media can, and often do, affect boys' sexual socialization. But media is just one element of the culture that surrounds boys. That culture—the "enduring behaviors, ideas, attitudes, and traditions shared by a large group of people and transmitted from one generation to the next"[10]—also includes parents and peers, two groups of people who play a significant role in shaping a boy's understanding and reception of media messages about sex. This book considers the influence of all three—media, parents, and peers—as it guides parents to a better understanding of how and where their sons learn about sex. It discusses the various issues facing boys and concludes with some tips and advice for parents and caregivers.

In *Boys, Sex & Media* I look primarily at boys in the middle- and high-school years, sharing research on how sexualized media affect their current and future attitudes about sex and sexual roles. Although boys may not become fully physically mature until well into their teenage years, messages about sex can reach them at a significantly younger age so a wide age range is important here.

Sexualized media have a decidedly heterosexual focus and so does this book. This is not to suggest that homosexuality has no place in a discussion of boys and sexualized media, but that the unique concerns of gay teens are outside the scope of this book. That being said, the examination of sexual health and body image in *Boys, Sex & Media* applies to boys of all sexual orientations.

In researching *Boys, Sex & Media*, I put my degree in library and information science to good use, scouring academic journals in a variety of disciplines for recent articles about sexualized media, masculinity, pornography, body image, sexual harassment, rape culture and myths, and sexual objectification of both sexes. I also studied psychological and communications theories about media impact on attitudes and behaviour, and the role parents and peers play in preventing negative media messages from taking root. My research is focused predominantly in North America, but also includes studies and news stories from the UK, Europe, and Australia.

A British MP once said "parents are powerless" against sexualized media.[11] That is not true. The goal of this book is to show parents exactly how much power they have, even against the seemingly endless tide of sexual content that threatens daily to overwhelm their sons.

Chapter 1—The Implicit Meanings in Explicit Content

> "In our culture, sex is becoming more and more visible, and more explicit."[1]
>
> *Feona Attwood*

It is hard to argue with this statement by Feona Attwood, a media and communications professor who studies sex in contemporary culture. The adjectives "explicit" and "visible" were well chosen: together they provide a very accurate summary of the current, sexualized state of our media and wider culture.

Greater openness about sexuality is not necessarily a bad thing. Positive, age-appropriate sexual materials, delivered in the right context, are especially good for teens trying to make sense of their emerging sexuality. Unfortunately, with producers and celebrities increasingly relying on twerk-and-grind imagery and excessive displays of skin to attract attention, much of the sexual content in today's popular culture is both negative in tone and inappropriate for the ever younger audiences that encounter it.

It is not just the visibility and explicit nature of sexual content that is of concern, but also the implicit messages this content delivers about sex and sexual roles. Pop culture depictions of sexuality are dominated by stereotyped views of gender, traditional notions of male-female sexual relationships (known in academic circles as the heterosexual script), and sexual objectification of women. These three elements pervade the media aimed at adolescents and perpetuate some very harmful ideas about male and female sexuality. They also provide a foundation for the issues discussed in the remainder of the book, so I will take some time to define them here.

Gender Stereotypes

If we dig deeply enough into the negative messages in sexualized media, we can see that gender stereotypes are at their root.

When we are born, we have no idea what it means to be a boy or a girl. Traditional notions about gender, long-established in our culture and passed onto us by the adults in our lives, provide lessons in how to be "appropriately" masculine or feminine.

In most Western countries, traditional views of masculinity define boys and men as naturally rational, assertive, aggressive, tough, competitive, and possessing physical, mental, and social strength and power. This masculine ideal holds the highest value in our society. Boys and men might not follow its every rule, but it is the standard against which they are measured and to which they compare themselves.

Traditional femininity positions women quite differently from men. They are considered gentler and more emotional than men, passive, weaker, less assertive, and more inclined toward restraint and self-denial. [2] (These attitudes persist despite societal shifts that show more women taking on the role of breadwinner[3,4] and more men acting less as provider and protector of the family and more as partner in life and parenting.)

These socially constructed ideals of masculinity and femininity tell teens what their response should be to their sexual urges and how they should behave in a sexual relationship: boys, as aggressive and physical beings, should pursue sex with lusty vigour and confidence; girls, excessively emotional and less tempted by carnal desires, should choose love and commitment over down-and-dirty sex.

A boy's gender socialization begins early and often lays the groundwork for his future attitudes toward sexual roles and dating. The trajectory starts in the preschool and primary grades, when girls and boys receive very different messages about what their gender means, and continues to the pre-teen and teen years where lessons learned in childhood are reinforced in the media and culture that surround boys.

Consider the most basic aspect of childhood: play. While many girls and boys today are comfortable playing with a wide range of toys—girls with building toys, boys with kitchens and baby dolls—there is one particular type of imaginary play targeted to girls exclusively: "pretty play."

This kind of play involves girls dressing up as princesses or pageant queens, putting on makeup, accessorizing with jewellery, pretending to enjoy a spa day, or playing with high-heeled, mini-skirted, often sexualized dolls that emphasize fashion and having the right look. The toys used in this kind of play place an emphasis on appearance that is absent from toys targeted to boys. A boy who dresses up as Iron Man or a police officer is doing so to play an active role, not to be admired or gazed upon as a princess or pageant participant might.

Unwitting adults add to the problem by complimenting girls, but not boys, on their appearance and making fashion and shopping a focus for their daughters but not their sons. The differences in treatment are not lost on children and can affect behaviour and attitudes. Many young girls develop a concern for appearance that boys of the same age simply do not. For their part, boys see the considerable effort girls put into being "pretty" and may begin to view that trait as far more important than the other attributes girls might possess, setting the stage for future evaluations of their female peers and the development of the so-called male gaze.

Another narrative that runs through the culture of young children is boy-as-hero. Many pop culture vehicles show males in the leadership or hero role, whether in the superhero genre itself, in male-dominated cartoon franchises, or video games. (The latter category includes one of the most egregious examples: Princess Peach from the *Super Mario* franchise, the damsel in distress who is in constant need of rescue by Mario.) Part and parcel of the male hero role is the diminishing of relationships. Unlike many female characters who worry over husbands or boyfriends, busy male heroes do not have time to think about love and romance. While there may be nothing overtly sexual in the male hero and lovestruck female tropes geared to younger children, they do reinforce stereotypical notions of men as less vested in their emotions and relationships.

Other stereotypes start young and can affect boys' later sexual socialization. Stoicism is one of them. It is seen every time an adult exhorts a boy not to cry or tells him to "suck it up" or "act like a man." The message is loud and clear. If you are a boy, you need to deal with your problems in silence; you do not cry or talk about what is bothering you. As boys enter their pre-teen and teenage years, this stereotype can be particularly damaging. Boys who are discouraged from talking about life in general may become reluctant to talk about matters sexual. In our rather uptight culture, sexuality is a hard subject for any young person to broach; being male just makes it that much harder. Male independence is another stereotype that comes into play here. Boys raised to believe they should never ask for help may refrain from asking questions about sex so they can maintain an air of self-sufficiency and prove they are man enough to figure out sex on their own.

Physical ideals are also rooted in stereotypes of men as strong and dominant. In recent years, there has been more emphasis on the perfect male form in media. This shift has had an impact on boys' body image and their perceptions of what makes men attractive. Hint: a 6-pack is often part of the package.

As boys get older, they are introduced to another idea that is based in gender stereotypes but has a more direct impact on sexual socialization: the heterosexual script.

Heterosexual Script

Sociologists refer to scripts as programs for behaviour that are learned early in life. People store these scripts in their memory and use them to guide their actions.[5] Sexual scripts give people cues about how to behave in a sexual relationship and what to expect from a sexual partner. Among sexual scripts in our culture, the heterosexual script trumps all others.

The heterosexual script is based heavily on traditional (and stereotyped) gender roles. In this script, sexual exploration is considered perfectly acceptable for assertive, physical, and inherently sexual males, but not for supposedly passive and self-denying women. Instead of being "players" like the guys, women and girls are expected to act as sexual gatekeepers, enforcing limits on sex and even their own desires. The imbalance in the script is even seen in the slang we use to describe sexual experience: males with a lot of "conquests" are praised as studs, while women who "get around" are considered sluts, tramps, or whores.

This double standard does not just affect girls, but also boys who do not conform to the stereotype. As psychologist Michael Wiederman notes, a boy who expresses doubt or a lack of sexual interest may have his masculinity questioned[6] since, according to the script, he is supposed to seek sex at every opportunity.

As described by psychologist Deborah Tolman and colleagues, the heterosexual script teaches people that sexuality carries different meanings and consequences for boys and girls. It consists of three major elements:

- sexual double-standards which state that sexual desire and experience are appropriate and normal for males but not for females who risk losing their "good girl" status if they appear sexually assertive;
- courtship strategies in which males are active and open in their pursuit of sex and females are far more passive and subtle;
- attitudes toward commitment where girls seek out faithfulness and devotion in their romantic and sexual relationships and boys choose to play the field.

In our popular culture, male characters enact this script by actively pursuing sex, sexually objectifying women, avoiding commitment, and taking the lead in sexual encounters. Female characters act out their part in the heterosexual script by using passive strategies to attract males (waiting to be asked out, exploiting their looks), seeking relationships instead of casual sexual encounters, and setting limits on sexual relationships; that is, fulfilling their role as sexual gatekeepers.[7]

The film *Don Jon* presents extreme cases of each. Lead male Jon is a serial seducer of women who boasts to his friends about his string of weekly conquests. Jon is also addicted to pornography, finding it far more satisfying than "real pussy." He eventually falls for Barbara, a woman who loves romantic films and believes that "real" men, motivated by love, will do whatever a woman wants. She refuses sex with Jon until he has demonstrated his commitment to her by enrolling in a college course to better himself, meeting her family, and bringing her home to meet his parents.[8] With its R-rating and serious subject matter it is doubtful that many adolescents will see the film, but it provides an excellent, if deliberately exaggerated, example of the heterosexual script for adults to consider.

The idea of male insatiability, in clear evidence in *Don Jon*, is also built into the heterosexual script. Psychologist Janna L. Kim and colleagues note that males often present their sexual feelings as uncontrollable, while women may try to appear less interested in sex and not prioritize their sexual desire. This element of the script may be slowly changing as more films and television programs show women wanting and pursuing sex, but the feminine ideal is still associated with a more chaste and patient approach to sex. News headlines of young women taking their lives after being bullied for "slutty" behaviour, cited in the introduction to this book, demonstrate all too clearly that this "purity myth"[9] is still a strong cultural force.

What is the danger of the heterosexual script? Kim and colleagues believe it may normalize traditional attitudes toward male and female sexual roles. The normality of the heterosexual script may also mean that many adults fail to notice its strong presence in teen media:

> Indeed, it is because the Heterosexual Script is so invisible and perceived to be so natural and normal that its potential impact on adolescents' sexual decision-making is so formidable.[10]
> (Capitalization present in the original.)

In other words, although it goes largely unnoticed, the heterosexual script can teach teens a lot about how to behave and what to expect in a sexual or romantic relationship. The lessons are not all positive. As we have seen here, the script reinforces many sexual stereotypes: promiscuous studs versus good girls, females valued for their appearance and openly objectified by males, and, in the words of psychologist L. Monique Ward, men as "sex-driven creatures who have trouble being faithful."

For boys, the script can also reinforce the wider cultural message that sexual experience is central to their masculinity—that the more sex they have, the more manly they are. On the other hand, by implying that turning sex down will make them less masculine, the heterosexual script can deny boys their sexual agency, making them feel as though they have no choice but to say "yes" even if they would rather say "no." [11]

The heterosexual script is conveyed not only through the behaviour exhibited in popular culture, but also through the objectifying imagery in our media environment.

Sexual Objectification

Sexual objectification is often misunderstood. Many people confuse "erotic" with "objectifying," believing that any time skin is shown, a person is being objectified. While that is often the case, it is not always so. Sexual objectification is not present in every sexual image or narrative. It occurs only when a person is "treated as a body (or collection of body parts)"[12] or dehumanized and made into a thing for others' sexual use.[13]

Sexual objectification takes many forms:

- Minimizing of a person's individuality. Faces might be removed or obscured so the person in a photograph or video is seen simply as a body. This trait is closely related to the concept of "reducing to body" or identifying a person solely in terms of their body or body parts. For women, the focus is normally the bottom, cleavage, or legs. For men it is the chest, bottom, and genital area.
- Violability, or making a person appear vulnerable. The subject—invariably a woman—may be positioned below the camera in a reclining or submissive position, with her legs spread open or clothes being pulled off.
- Silencing, which is generally accomplished by removing a face or head, reinforcing the idea that a person is to be gazed upon but not have any agency of his or her own.[14]

Subordination is another potential sign of objectification. In the 1970s sociologist Erving Goffman talked about the "ritualization of subordination," a phrase he coined to describe the ways advertisements featuring men and women use body positioning and posing to reinforce ideas about gender and, depending on the content of the ad, sexual roles. Men leaning over women, physically dominating the space, or exerting some kind of control over a woman who is lying down or in another position of submission are hallmarks of the ritualization of subordination. Submissive poses include:

- Recumbent positions which, at the time Goffman wrote, were more typical among female models than male. Goffman believed this position signalled sexual availability and hinted at the violability mentioned above, since someone who is lying down is less capable of initiating "physical defense of oneself." This pose is still very common in advertising today.
- Bashful knee bend, in which a woman is standing a bit off-balance, making her seem a less forceful presence.
- Canting postures, which involve twisting or bending the body away from the camera or lowering the head, denoting submissiveness, subordination, and appeasement.

Sexually objectifying images are common in media, especially in the world of advertising.

Clothier American Apparel had been one of the worst offenders until its bankruptcy filing in October, 2015.[15] The restructuring forced the company to take a look at all of its operations, including, apparently, its advertising. New CEO Paula Schneider noted in 2015 that she was seeking a way to "keep American Apparel's grittiness" while getting rid of imagery that was "totally over the line,"[16] a phrase that describes a rather large swath of the company's advertising output over the past ten years.

An ad from December, 2013 typifies the American Apparel approach. Although promoting underwear, this print ad did it in a very objectifying manner, showing a woman's bum—and only her bum—as she leaned over a bed, with the sheer underwear leaving precious little to the imagination.[17] In fact, the company's entire archive features a dizzying array of similar shots: spread-eagle or bum-up women reclining on beds or floors, looking vulnerable and overtly sexualized with their faces often not shown. Objectifying imagery also appeared in a late 2014 campaign by designer Alexander Wang which showed a female model lying with her head back and eyes closed, naked, save for the jeans scrunched around the bottom of her legs.[18] The advertisement was ostensibly about jeans but the model's apparel was clearly never intended to be the focal point. In late 2015, I Love Ugly—a retailer of men's clothing in New Zealand—made headlines around the world for its sexual objectification of women. To promote a new line of men's jewellery, the company photographed men's hands laden with rings, but placed those hands a naked woman's breasts, bum, and vaginal area. The focus was entirely on the woman's various parts, turning her body into a plaything instead of presenting her as a full human being.[19]

It is not just the fashion industry that is culpable either. American restaurant chain Carl's Jr. has taken sexual objectification to new depths, routinely zooming in on the cleavage, legs, and lips of the bikini-clad models who star in the company's commercials. And then there is Hooters, where objectification is built right into the name and present throughout its marketing. A pair of television ads from 2014 featured the Hooters girls being run through some football-styled drills by former NFL coach Jon Gruden. Slow motion is used to highlight bouncing breasts as the voiceover notes that Hooters girls make football more fun to watch.[20]

As I noted earlier, however, not all sexy images are objectifying. Consider a well-known campaign by fast-fashion retailer H&M. Designed to market the company's line of men's underwear, the ads featured a muscular and bare-chested David Beckham standing upright and staring into the camera. Mr. Beckham's body was being used to sell a product, but his ads were not objectifying to the same degree as those described above. His posture and direct gaze did not imply submissiveness, a loss of autonomy, or violability, and, with his highly recognizable face fully visible, his individuality was not in question.

This contrast between images that are sexual and those that are sexually objectifying is important to note. Men may be showing more skin in popular culture, but that does not necessarily translate into sexual objectification. Although there is a shift occurring, in many cases, barely-dressed men are posed in ways that demonstrate their physical power. When women are eroticized they are often objectified as well, reduced to body parts (typically breasts and bottom), and posed to look seductive and available or even vulnerable and violable.

Repeated viewing of sexually objectifying images of women can affect young men's attitudes, strengthening their belief in stereotyped gender roles and making them more likely to view women only as sex objects.[21]

Is the impact of male sexual objectification the same? No one knows the answer to that question yet. There are relatively fewer instances of men being sexually objectified in our culture, so there is less research into the possible impact of such treatment. But men are not getting off scot-free either. Whether or not they objectify, sexualized images contribute to the distorted body ideals that have become standards of attractiveness in our society. Such images focus on one body type for each sex—lean and muscular for men, slim and buxom for women—while also sending the message that the body is the most important gauge of a person's attractiveness and worth. In a sexualized media environment, sexual appeal takes on greater importance and people swayed by media messages (including men) may begin to see themselves as less desirable if they do not conform to societal ideals of perfect, sexy bodies.

What Does It All Mean?

Gender stereotypes and the heterosexual script are well established in our media and wider culture and remarkably persistent, despite changes in the economic and family roles played by men and women. From the time they are very young, boys are immersed in gender stereotypes, learning that the ideal male is strong, independent, and not prone to excessive displays of emotion. As boys get older, these familiar notions collide with social norms about male-female relationships to create a picture of males as sexually assertive and entitled to act on their urges in ways that females cannot. Objectification sets up a view of women as something to be visually consumed, evaluated in terms of sexual appeal, and, in extreme cases, used only for sexual gratification.

Together, these elements—gender stereotypes, the heterosexual script, and sexual objectification—exert a powerful influence on boys' understanding of male sexuality. The strength of these elements is reinforced by their ubiquity, with all three appearing regularly in media rated from PG to R and, of course, X.

Chapter 2—Pornography: The "Elephant on the Screen"

> "…pornography is a prominent feature of the current emerging adulthood culture."[1]
>
> *Jason S. Carroll*

Pornography has become a fact of life for many adolescents, as sociologist Jason S. Carroll notes in the passage above, but the jury is still out on its potential ramifications.

Sociologist Marshall Smith coined the phrase "the elephant on the screen," used in the title of this chapter. In 2008 he wrote that sexually explicit material (SEM) could influence adolescents' sexual beliefs and behaviours, but "a consensus has not emerged as to the effects."[2] Other researchers argue that the impact of porn on pre-teens and teens is decidedly negative.

So, which is it: harmful or benign? This question is of great concern to many parents worried about the potentially corrupting influence of pornography on teenage boys. I will shed some light on the subject here, looking at how we got to the point of free, 24-7 access to X-rated films, what boys are seeing when they watch online pornography, and the possible consequences of porn use.

How Did We Get Here?

With videos entitled "12 inches of black meat in Monica," and "Wonder Woman getting her pussy pounded by Captain America,"[3] it is tempting to believe that today's porn is some kind of aberration; a sign of the depravity that characterizes certain elements of our media (among which I include most of reality TV). While it's true that much of today's pornography has taken a violent and misogynistic turn, some acts considered extreme these days actually have a long history.

Erotic imagery dates as far back as the Paleolithic period, where small sculptures of women with greatly exaggerated breasts and hips were created, likely to celebrate female fertility.[4] Ancient Greek and Roman art highlighted the phallus, sometimes to arouse, but also to worship "the powers of creativity that the sexual organ represents."[5] (That the Greeks were more fluid in their sexuality and known for their unequal treatment of women[6] may also have contributed to this phallus worship.)

Since ancient times, artists have produced great volumes of erotic paintings, sketches, and sculptures. Pieces created for the sole purpose of sexual arousal were typically a private indulgence. It was only after the arrival of the printing press that wide distribution of erotic art became possible.

One of the earliest collections of erotic art was *I Modi*, published in 1524. Its explicit depictions of sexual positions earned it the enmity of the Vatican. Eventually all copies were destroyed[7] but the genie was out of the bottle. Artists from that point forward flouted the laws of the Church and continued to produce extremely explicit images. Group sex, large orgies, and a wide variety of sexual positions were common in the erotic art of the 17th and 18th centuries.[8]

Advancements in the printing process led to the emergence of written erotica which first appeared in English in the 1660s.[9] Like the visual artists who preceded them, the creators of this early erotica did not hold back. *The Memoirs of a Woman of Pleasure*, also known as *Fanny Hill*, was written in 1749 and is perhaps one of the best known erotic novels from the period. In rather florid language, it describes sexual encounters between two women, masturbation, voyeurism, various sexual positions, and the considerable physical endowments of the men Fanny meets. The following passage, in which Fanny surreptitiously watches a couple engage in the act, is one of the tamest in the book:

> "Her sturdy stallion had now unbuttoned, and produced naked, stiff and erect, that wonderful machine, which I had never seen before, and which, for the interest my own seat of pleasure began to take furiously in it, I stared at with all the eyes I had…"[10]

It was steamy stuff, despite the fancy language.

A half-century later, the notorious Marquis de Sade would publish his erotic novel *Juliette*. Its text and illustrations depicted practices like spanking and bondage that would later become known as sadomasochism (S&M). Along with the author's libertine philosophy, the book also included liberal use of the words "fuck" and "cunt," explicit descriptions of the positions of each player in the various orgies that take place, anal and oral sex, and multiple penetration of women by men, dildos, or strap-ons[11]—all hallmarks of today's pornography.

Those themes carried into early 20th century pornographic photographs and films.[12] Still shots from the period include S&M[13] and a great variety of sexual positions. Save for their grainy quality, early pornographic films depict scenes similar to some of the tamer porn seen today—nuns in an abbey getting it on with a abbot and a priest, female students being disciplined at school as a pretext for a sexual encounter that includes plenty of consensual spanking, and lots of group and oral sex.[14] (The short films I saw were part of a compilation entitled *The Good Old Naughty Days* which also includes scenes of bestiality.)

Clearly, explicit depictions of sex—even practices that are still considered unorthodox today—have been with us for a long time.

So why the hand-wringing over pornography in the 21st century? The answer is probably obvious, but I will state it for the record: concerns today centre on the easy accessibility, ubiquity, and gender bias in current hardcore representations of sex which, because of technology, reach even the youngest among us, unfiltered and unfettered.

Whereas the porn of yesteryear was restricted to brothels, in the case of the films in *The Good Old Naughty Days*, or retailers of adults-only products, today it is available with the click of a mouse. With the Internet, boys can circumvent all of the limits that restricted previous generations from viewing XXX videos, and watch what they want, when they want, and wherever they want, thanks to mobile devices.

As for what they are watching, the answer varies depending on the person. Sexually explicit media may be easily accessible, but not all boys are indulging. Still, a significant number are and for very good reason: as they mature both physically and emotionally, they become curious about what sex is and how it is done. To satisfy this normal, natural interest in sexuality, some will seek out explicit videos, often for their own enjoyment but also to save themselves the embarrassment of having to ask someone else about sex.

This interest in sex is healthy but what boys find online may not be. The concern is not so much with boys seeing sex performed but with the ways in which sex is presented. Media depictions of explicit sex tend to follow traditional sexual scripts, showing the man as the dominant player in pursuit of attractive and acquiescent, even submissive, women. Some porn takes it even further, treating women with aggression or violence and even portraying sex as an act of anger.

Who Is Watching Porn and What Are They Seeing?

Pornography has been defined as "explicit representation of sexual acts with visible genitalia," with the intention to arouse. Pornography is considered distinct from soft-core content which does not generally include visible sex organs.[15] Historian Sarah Toulalan notes that in the modern context, pornography is very much a part of visual culture, seen in "images of naked bodies and sexual activity as presented in magazines, films, and videos and, most particularly now, on the Internet." [16]

While it is true that the Internet—"present and prioritized in the lives of many youth"[17]—has made pornography widely available to teens, its usage is not universal in this age group.

The statistics on teen use of pornography vary greatly, depending on the country of origin and the methodology used to determine the numbers:

- Security software vendor GFI commissioned Knowledge Networks to prepare a parent-teen Internet safety report in 2011. The US-based study showed that 31% of surveyed boys admitted to visiting adult websites and 13% said they do so "often" or "sometimes."[18]
- A 2008 YouGov study reported by Britain's Channel 4 indicated that 42% of sexually active teens use porn regularly: more than a quarter of surveyed boys reported using porn at least once a week and 5% reported using it every day.[19]
- A 2008 study by social psychologist Chiara Sabina and colleagues asked college students about their use of porn during their

adolescent years. Most had accessed porn for the first time between the ages of 14 and 17, with some seeing it for the first time at age 12 (10.9%) or 13 (16%). Overall, 93.2% of males had seen porn before the age of 18 compared to 62.1% of females.[20]

- In 2009, journalism professor Jane D. Brown and behavioural scientist Kelly L'Engle reported that 53% of males had reported using sexually explicit media at least once in the previous year, compared to 28% of females. [21]
- Telecommunications professor Paul J. Wright and colleagues found in a 2012 study that 17% of the websites visited by teens are X-rated and at least 6% contain sexual violence.[22]
- In 2009, a study from security software company Symantec showed that among children's top ten Internet search terms, "sex" ranked fourth, closely followed by "porn" in sixth place.[23]

From these numbers, it seems that sexually curious boys are seeking out pornography, but many are not regular users. Indeed, some of the highest percentages, like those indicated by Brown and L'Engle and Sabina, do not refer to regular use but rather to sporadic use of as little as one time during a given period. Still, porn use could be a problem for some boys: many are seeing pornography at very young ages and even the 5% in Britain who use it every day constitute a rather large number in that population.[24] And it is boys who stand to be most directly influenced by porn. As sociologist Michael Flood notes and other studies also show, males are more likely "to use pornography, to do so repeatedly, to use it for sexual excitement and masturbation, to initiate its use (rather than be introduced to it by an intimate partner), to view it alone and in same-sex groups, and to view more types of images."[25]

Statistics on the gender differences in porn use vary, but a 2012 study by communications scholar Mathias Weber and colleagues indicates that, among teenage respondents to their study, only 3% of females watched porn on a daily basis, compared to 47% of males. Overall, only 2% of boys in his survey had never seen porn compared to 19% of girls. Other studies show similar ratios, with porn viewing an overwhelmingly male pastime.

The Sabina study looked into the reasons teens use porn. Among boys, the majority wanted sexual excitement (69.3%), but 53.1% said they used it out of curiosity about "different things people do sexually," and 39.7% said they wanted information about sex.

These results are echoed in Weber's study which suggested that teens use pornography not only for arousal, but also to discover sexual behaviour and explore their own sexual preferences. As Weber and colleagues note, pornographic films are the only place sexually curious teens can see sex, so it stands to reason that they will seek them out.[26]

A 2009 study from Sweden drew conclusions similar to Weber's. This survey of Swedish youth aged 14 -20 found that male adolescents use porn for arousal and sexual information (positions, new techniques), and that teens in general use porn as a form of social intercourse. They watch together to gauge peer reactions to what is seen on screen, thereby discovering the "normative guidelines" of their peer group.[27]

In short, teens use pornography for information about sex, not just titillation, a fact noted by pediatricians Debra Braun-Courville and Mary Rojas who believe that mass media in general play an important role in the sexual socialization of youth, but the Internet may be at the forefront. Indeed, for boys, the Internet is the most popular choice for viewing sexually explicit media, favoured by 40%, followed by X-rated DVDs at 36% and pornographic magazines at 29%.[28]

Braun-Courville and Rojas also cite research showing why the Internet has become so important: it is affordable, accessible, and anonymous.[29] Teens can access it anywhere for free without having to reveal who they are or what they have been watching. Mobile devices have increased this sense of freedom, making teen online activity "portable" and also "largely unmonitored."[30]

Most parents are aware that porn is easily accessible but may not be as familiar with the actual content. As social psychologist Gail Dines says in her book *Pornland*, most women and some men have an idea of pornography that is twenty years out of date.[31]

Before researching this book, I would have fallen into that category myself. While I am no expert, I have done a brief survey of pornography through the ages and can make something of a comparison to current porn. As I said earlier, the actual sex acts have not changed much but the tone has. In the older videos and images I saw, women were often portrayed as enjoying sex and participating equally in what was happening. In a lot of today's porn—or at least much of what I saw on free porn sites and the sites associated with porn magazines—women are routinely objectified and sex is depicted with a high degree of hostility; something men do *to* women, not *with* them. For their part, the women seem to acquiesce to whatever the men want, making sex about fulfilling men's needs, not women's. (For the record, porn targeted to women, sometimes called erotica, offers a much more balanced depiction, with the women enjoying themselves as much as the men.)

Examples of fairly typical X-rated content can be found on the websites of pornographic magazines, although online access to North America's big three X-rated publications varies. *Playboy*, which announced in October, 2015 that it would end "full nudity" in its print magazine,[32] still offers plenty of skin on its *Playboy Plus* website. Most of the content appears to be behind a paywall but clickable links at the bottom of the main page grant access to galleries like "Playmates," "Amateurs," and "Coeds." The latter category promises "fun coed girls" that will "get down & naughty," along with "fresh teen faces" who "bare it all,"[33] while the "Special Edition" area of the site offers "hot girl on girl action."[34] Each category includes several pages of images, but most are pretty tame compared to the *Penthouse* and *Hustler* sites. At penthouse.com visitors will get an eyeful of still images taken from their videos of couples engaging in the act. Over at *Hustler*, the raunchiest of the three magazines, a lot of explicit content is available via nude galleries and video previews. To access this content, a site visitor simply has to click "yes" when asked if he or she is 18 or older. The video previews are usually under two minutes in length but make the most of that short time by including a tightly edited montage of all kinds of sex acts, especially women performing oral sex on a man or another woman, "money shots" of men reaching orgasm in a woman's mouth, and lots of close-ups of hard-driving intercourse that looks painful for the women involved. And this is not even the worst.

My March, 2013 search for "free porn" on Google resulted in 724,000,000 hits. A similar search in December, 2015 found fewer hits overall, but still listed 213,000,000 links. Both searches led to www.xnxx.com, a site that in 2013 included video clips with titles like "Jizz on her pretty face," "Hot and horny girlfriend get anal on couch," and "Naughty Wife Punished Hard." Newer titles, seen in 2015, include "Teen tries her biggest dick ever," "Brother Tricks Sister into Anal," and "Ebony slut in an amazing gang bang." Some of the videos on the site appear to offer more tepid depictions of sex but a look at the categories in the sidebar showed all manner of positions and several options for viewing aggressive sex: choices include gangbang, gagging, deepthroat, and throat-fucking.[35] The oral fixation of the latter three themes is also present in the imagery on the *Hustler* site, where women are routinely pictured with absolutely huge penises being thrust into their mouths.

Hustler is certainly not the place one would expect to find gender balance or any kind of enlightened attitude toward women, but much of its content goes beyond basic male sexual dominance into cruelty and degradation. Consider a still shot from January, 2015 showing a woman with black eye makeup running down her face, either from crying or semen, as she attempts to wrap her mouth around an absurdly huge penis. Or the promo for a video called *Four-Eyed Fuck Fest*, centred on sex with women wearing glasses and stating that "when you're ready to pop, make sure you give these spectacle-wearing sluts a big load of ball juice—right in their luscious lenses." And on, and on, with references to sluts and whores, pussies and snatch, cum facials, *Teen Anal Pounding*, and Latinas who like "to get their holes stretched and pounded." Sadly, violence and porn often go together and the images and language seen on the *Hustler* site, while shocking for those unaccustomed to porn, are not at all atypical. In fact, some porn goes even further.

Dines notes the role of the profit motive in the shift to more extreme acts in pornographic films—with so many players in the field, each has to find new ways to attract an audience, and what used to be considered hard-core is now mainstream. One example is "ass-to-mouth" or ATM, a sex act in which a man puts his penis in a woman's anus and then into her mouth (another category on xnxx.com). According to research cited by psychologist John D. Foubert, ATM scenes occur in 41% of pornographic films.[36]

In her book, Dines talks about a particular subgenre of porn called "gonzo" which is characterized by tremendous brutality and abuse of women.

According to Dines, gonzo is the "overwhelmingly dominant porn genre" because it focuses on sex and not narrative, making it cheaper to produce. (Narrative has never been a major concern in standard porn, but it is, apparently, even less of a focus in gonzo.) In the gonzo genre, women are penetrated simultaneously in different orifices by multiple male partners, sometimes sustaining injuries, or gagged to the point of vomiting when performing oral sex.

As the examples above demonstrate, most porn takes to extreme the sexual script of men as dominant and women as compliant partners seeking to please a man. In the porn version of this script, women suffer immensely. They are shown as submissive and accepting of whatever men want; less people than instruments for a man, or men's, sexual gratification.

And what of the men in porn? They are the perpetrators of some truly sickening acts of aggression against women. It may be hard to have much sympathy for them, but Dines notes that, like their female counterparts, porn men are portrayed in a negative and one-dimensional manner: "…as soulless, unfeeling, amoral life-support systems for erect penises who are entitled to use women in any way they want. These men demonstrate zero empathy, respect, or love for the women they have sex with."[37] That the men themselves express no enjoyment or even response until the moment of ejaculation is another sign of their lack of emotional investment. Media and communications professor Feona Attwood notes that these men are presented as little more than machines that "shoot massive jets of come" but get little else out of their sexual encounters.[38] Given the horrible things done to women in some porn, the idea of men being objectified and dehumanized might sound ridiculous, but not to Dines and other researchers. They believe porn men bear signs of objectification since the focus is not on them as people but on one specific part of their bodies.

The Impact of Porn on Boys

It is easy to be outraged by pornography, but is there reason to worry about its effect on boys, many of whom use as it a sexual education tool or an arbiter of what is acceptable or normal in a sexual relationship?

Some say there is little cause for concern. Swedish research, cited earlier, indicates that porn is becoming more socially acceptable and an integral part of an adolescent's everyday life. Although the study used a very small sample of teens, its authors concluded that the majority of participants had acquired the necessary skills "to navigate the pornographic landscape in a sensible and reflective manner," noting that male and female participants seemed equally cognizant of the gender inequities in porn and equally aware that the sex shown in porn videos is exaggerated, distorted, or false.[39]

Teens themselves have been asked their thoughts. Many describe pornography use as normal and even positive. Marshall Smith notes that boys see porn as a way of learning new techniques or "tricks,"[40] while Weber and colleagues described porn use as "socially desirable" in some peer groups and a tool for achieving or maintaining status within that group.[41]

It all sounds very shiny and happy. In reality, the long-term effects of adolescent pornography use are not yet known, despite what teens and some researchers might think.

Much of the research into the impacts of porn focuses on adults, not children and teens. Because children are accessing sexually explicit videos and being exposed to porn-inspired imagery in music videos and other media at increasingly younger ages—and at crucial periods when their sexual attitudes and scripts are being formed—research on this age group is badly needed. It is, however, very hard to conduct. The most accurate research comes from lab-controlled experiments which would require children and young teens to sit in a room and watch sexually explicit media. Clearly such experiments are unethical. Instead of laboratory studies, researchers are using surveys of teens and pre-teens to determine the extent of pornography use and its possible impacts. The results may be somewhat less accurate but are still enlightening.

Psychologists Jochen Peter and Patti Valkenburg are among the most prolific researchers in this area, having written extensively about adolescent use of "sexually explicit Internet media" (SEIM), a term they prefer over the emotionally charged word "pornography."[42] Their body of research shows how SEIM affects adolescents and explains why its effects can be so strong. Where most people, including the mainstream media, think that porn's influence on males is manifested in increased sexual aggression and objectification of women, Peter and Valkenburg show that the impact might be deeper and more insidious.

In 2008, Peter and Valkenburg found that frequent use of SEIM led to more thoughts about sex, stronger interest in it—beyond the "sexual curiosity that characterizes adolescence"—and more frequent instances of teens being distracted by their thoughts about sex. In their words, "SEIM leaves its traces in adolescents' thinking about sex."[43]

Those traces can be fairly significant. As we saw earlier, adolescents tend to use SEIM as a tool for sex education. Its educational impact is not just on the act itself, but also on fundamental attitudes.

At the core are the concepts of perceived realism and perceived utility. In a 2010 study, Peter and Valkenburg concluded that more frequent use of SEIM among teens leads to a greater belief that these materials are socially realistic and useful for learning about sex. In turn, teens who hold those beliefs tend to develop a more instrumental attitude toward sex; that is, a notion that sex is "a primarily physical, casual game" with a person's sexual pleasure deemed more important than relationships, connection, and affection.[44]

Similar conclusions were made in another 2008 study. Although it focused on emerging adults aged 18-26 and not younger teens, this study showed that young people do not necessarily need to use porn to be accepting of it and influenced by it. Participants in the study were asked whether they thought porn was an acceptable way to express their sexuality. Men who agreed with the statement—even if they did not use pornography themselves—tended to be more accepting of premarital and casual sex. This study demonstrates that even a cursory knowledge of pornography could have an impact on sexual attitudes, acting as a "value stance" or "sexual ethic."[45]

What is the problem with an instrumental attitude? Teens who take a more casual attitude to sex may put themselves at risk of sexually transmitted infections and the emotional health effects that come from promiscuous behaviour, a topic I will explore in greater detail in the next chapter.

Beyond fostering an acceptance of casual sex and promiscuity, pornography may have other negative impacts on boys' emerging sexuality.

Porn can affect boys' sexual scripts by altering their sense of what is realistic or expected in sexual encounters.[46] In particular, Marshall Smith believes pornography may reinforce the stereotypes of experienced,[47] sexually adventurous males and passive, accommodating females. This exaggerated heterosexual script, which is dominant in porn, may also diminish boys' sexual self-esteem and lead to sexual anxiety, as it presents a performance ideal for males (i.e. that they can go for hours) and positions men as initiators of sex who must have more sexual knowledge and skill than their female partners.

Pornography also blurs the lines about consent, an already hazy area for teens. In pornographic films, consent is never mentioned and sexual encounters escalate to extremes without discussion—women's bodies are explored and penetrated, additional men or women join, and men ejaculate all over women with nary an "Are you okay with this?" being asked.

Sociologist Michael Flood notes as well that porn and other sexually explicit media can lead to a wider acceptance of non-mainstream sexual acts, like anal or group sex. As we saw earlier in this chapter, these practices have been with us for a long time but they carry risks to sexual health if precautions are not taken, and in porn, they never are.

With the conflicting body of evidence about the impact of pornography, what conclusions can we draw? The news is both reassuring and worrisome. It is good to know the majority of boys are not regular users of porn—a fact not widely noted in media reports. Yet it is troubling to read about the subtle ways porn can shape boys' sexual scripts and the number of boys who see porn as a valuable educational resource. On that count, the words of psychologist Michael Flood seem particularly relevant. He noted in a 2009 paper that pornography is a poor sex educator—most is too explicit for young people, shows sex in unrealistic ways while neglecting intimacy, is sexist, and, in some cases, eroticizes violence.[48]

Yet boys clearly crave more information about sex, so what is the answer for parents? Sex education is very delicate issue, rooted in a family's morals and values. There is no one-size-fits-all solution. There are, however, some realities that all parents need to face in a media environment where sexualized imagery is becoming increasingly normalized and ubiquitous. It is not just pornography but other media that help shape boys' attitudes toward sex, including magazines and music videos that are increasingly adopting a porn aesthetic. In order to make the best decisions for their sons' sexual education and development, parents need to understand the possible influences of all sexualized media on boys' sexual health, notions of consent, experience of aggression, and body esteem.

Chapter 3—Swagger and Boys' Sexual Health

"What did you miss most, the alcohol or the meaningless sex?"[1]

-TV Program Arrow

The inquiry above was made of Oliver Queen (The Green Arrow) in the pilot episode of the popular series *Arrow* upon his return home from a five-year sojourn on a mostly deserted island. The question is loaded with implicit meaning about how males of a certain age are expected to approach sex: get drunk, get laid, no strings, no problems. The words of Oliver's friend are a sign of the swagger that dominates media depictions of the male sexual role. Portrayals like this help perpetuate the myth that boys possess an all-consuming sex drive and value physical gratification over messy emotions like love.

The reality is quite different. Michele Chai, a health promoter with Planned Parenthood in Toronto, talked about swagger in a widely read 2014 article in Canada's *The Walrus*:

> "People tend to think that the swagger young men display is because they have confidence about sex...You want to know the three things about sex that young guys lie about most often to their peers?...One, how often they have sex. Two, how much they enjoy the sex they actually have. And three, whether or not they use condoms."[2] [Condoms presumably contradicting the freewheeling approach to sex that signifies masculinity.]

Chai concluded her remarks by noting that swagger and the lies it spawns add up to too many unhappy and unsafe sexual encounters for boys.

Popular representations of adolescent boys and young men trade in swagger. Males are routinely shown as preoccupied with sex and women's bodies. The more timid among them ogle women from afar while others with more confidence confront women directly with a come-on or catcall. Representations like these are based in traditional and highly stereotyped views of male sexuality and masculinity. Pediatrician Mary Ott has talked about the impact of these stereotypes on boys: poor sexual health outcomes during adolescence and less engagement with healthcare services, especially as adolescent males enter adulthood. She notes as well that adolescent males who adhere to conventional beliefs about masculinity report more sexual partners, less intimate relationships during their last reported intercourse, less consistent condom use, and less belief in male responsibility to prevent pregnancy.[3]

The World Health Organization defines sexual health as "...a state of physical, emotional, mental and social well-being in relation to sexuality; it is not merely the absence of disease, dysfunction or infirmity."[4] As we will see, our society has a long way to go to ensure true sexual health for boys.

A Failure to Communicate

The acquisition of sexual health information (SHI) is vital to the sexual health of teen boys and girls. Armed with the facts, they are less vulnerable to infection, less likely to experience unwanted pregnancies, and more likely to share in healthy relationships. Yet, as Rachel Giese wrote in *The Walrus*, young straight men are the most ignored demographic when it comes to sexual health education.[5]

On the one hand, it is clear why sexual education is, in Giese's words, female-slanted: girls get pregnant and suffer far more incidents of sexual violence. But that narrow view is detrimental to boys and, by extension, the girls they date or "hook up" with. It takes two to tango, and if boys are not educated about their role in ensuring their own sexual health and that of their partner, both parties in the relationship lose.

There are three main sources of accurate SHI for boys: parents, teachers, and healthcare professionals. In a 2013 study, professor of pediatrics Abigail Donaldson found that sexual health lessons resonate more when they come from multiple sources. Her research also showed that teens view parents, teachers, and healthcare providers not only as important sources for this information, but preferred sources. Yet very few teens actually receive sexual health information from all three. In fact, many get it from only one source which may not provide a complete picture. A brief look at each source will show us where the gaps are and where boys turn to fill them.

When it comes to talking about sex, the parental relationship probably causes the most angst. Research shows that teens want to talk to their parents about sex and parents want to have those conversations, but neither party manages to find the words. Donaldson's study showed a startling lack of discussion between parents and their sexually experienced sons: 60% of these sexually active boys reported receiving no information about birth control from parents, compared to 33% of girls. Further, 48% of boys reported receiving no information on condoms, and 36% had been given no information about STI prevention.[6]

Why such a failure to communicate? One reason is general discomfort. Most teens find it difficult to talk to parents about sex, while parents are uncertain how to broach the subject.

Cultural forces might also be at play. Male stereotypes and the heterosexual script often dictate what parents discuss with their sons, if and when they have conversations about sex. If parents believe their sons should be independent and self-sufficient and girls are sexual gatekeepers, they may be less inclined to cover all the bases in sexual education.

Consider the example of pregnancy prevention. Recent numbers from the National Campaign to Prevent Teen Pregnancy show results similar to Donaldson's: 59% of sexually experienced boys had not talked to their parents about birth control, compared to 39% of sexually experienced girls. Further, only 29% of sexually experienced boys had talked to a parent about where to get birth control, compared to 49% of sexually experienced girls. Donaldson also found that 17% of boys had never received birth control information from parents or teachers, compared to 10% of girls. Clearly a significant number of parents believe girls are primarily responsible for pregnancy prevention and if parents buy into this notion, it is likely their sons will too. In reality, contraception use increases when *both* partners agree on the method, yet many boys lack the information to speak intelligently with their partners about birth control.

In the area of STIs, parents are a little more balanced in their approach. Donaldson found that about two-thirds of sexually experienced boys and girls had talked to their parents about STIs.[7,8]

Teachers are trying to do their part for sexual education when curricula allow them. As for effectiveness, it appears there is work to be done in the area of birth control education. A 2012 report by the Guttmacher Institute in the US showed that 46% of sexually experienced males (compared to 23% of females) had received no formal instruction from teachers about contraception before their first time having sexual intercourse.[9] Donaldson's 2013 report had a slightly different result, finding that 37% of boys had not received information about birth control from teachers, compared to 25% of girls. Both numbers are inexcusably high, indicating as they do that roughly 4 out of 10 boys are not learning about contraception at school.

The numbers are a little better on STI education in schools. The Guttmacher study notes that in the years between 2006 and 2008, most teens aged 15–19 had received formal instruction about STIs (93%) and HIV (89%). Donaldson's study showed similar results, with 96% of boys having received information about STI prevention from a teacher.

Despite these efforts, there is evidence that school-based sexual education is not as meaningful as it could be for boys. Rachel Giese wrote that with sexual education geared more toward girls, boys tend to find the lessons "irrelevant and boring." The timing might also be wrong: the male subjects in a 2008 study done by social work professor Jessica Ayala were unanimous in their opinion that sexual education in schools comes too late. They also expressed frustration with the "fear-based model" of sexual education employed by most schools, designed, as it is, to reduce risky sexual behaviour while disregarding the "sensual aspects" of sex.[10,11]

This doomsday approach is undoubtedly based in adults' erroneous fears that talking about sex—whether in a positive or negative sense—will encourage teens to have more sex. In reality, comprehensive sexual education has been shown to delay sexual initiation in most children.[12] Despite some parents' fears, sexual education is not the spark that ignites a teen's sex drive. Sex is an innate impulse and, at a certain age, every teenager gets wants to learn more about it. Even teens who are not sexually active have questions about sex, stemming from both their natural curiosity and their desire to be prepared for the time they shift from thinking about sex to actually doing it. Specifically, teens want to know more about: how to use condoms correctly; how sex, personal empowerment and happiness fit together; symptoms, testing, and treatment of STIs; and how to communicate with partners about sensitive sexual issues, including consent.[13] The latter topic could also include tips about how to say "no." The boys Giese talked to in *The Walrus* article also stated an interest in learning about healthy relationships and sexual pleasure—topics that are typically absent from school curricula.

The lack of effectiveness of school-based sexual education is not necessarily the fault of teachers. The curricula they are given can limit their options, especially in areas where abstinence education is mandated[14] or the fear-based model is the only choice available to them.

If parents are a tad squeamish, and teachers are limited by curricula, can doctors at least provide young men with the sexual health information they need? Apparently they are coming up short too.

In a 2012 report, pediatrician Arik Marcell noted that doctors frequently talk about sexual health with female patients but most fail to initiate discussions about sexual health with teen boys. His research showed that doctors are three times more likely to take sexual health histories from females than males, and twice as likely to counsel girls on the use of condoms.

Of course, doctors and other healthcare professionals cannot help boys if boys do not seek their care. For a variety of reasons, boys and young men tend not to access sexual health services. Conditioned to be stoic and self-sufficient, boys often feel too embarrassed to ask questions or talk about their sexuality. Some fear looking stupid and others worry they will appear unmanly if they ask for help, especially about sex. Sex role stereotypes also play a part in boys' reluctance to visit the doctor. Many young men believe there is no point in learning anything about sex because they are ultimately not responsible for the consequences of the act.[15] Ignorance is another reason boys stay away from the doctor. Few are aware of the health issues males face, which is not surprising given the general lack of attention to male reproductive health in our society. A lack of confidential services geared to boys is also a factor in the low use of health services by boys.[16]

The latter point was noted in reports by the National Campaign to Prevent

Teen Pregnancy. In 2006 studies, the organization drilled down into the numbers and found that while 53% of teen girls reported visiting a public health clinic for reproductive health services, only 19% of boys did. Other studies by the campaign have shown that boys tend to avoid sexual health programs at clinics because they are not male-friendly.[17]

As Marcell noted in his report, it is not just public health clinics that are failing boys. Among boys who went to a family doctor, the majority did not receive counselling or information about birth control or STIs. In fact, only 24% received any information about contraception or STI prevention, with slightly more (27%) being counselled about HIV/AIDS. Girls did not fare much better when it came to STI information, but many more girls (45%) received counselling about contraception.[18,19]

With tentative parents, boring sex ed classes, and too few health services, many sexually curious boys turn to alternate sources of information that are easily accessible but neither healthy nor completely factual. Pornography is one such source. As we saw in chapter 2, nearly 40% of boys who use XXX films use them to learn about sex.[20] Others seek answers to their sexual queries in movies, television, and magazines.

Friends are another "starting point" for boys' sexual education.[21] Boys often talk to their peers about pregnancy and STI prevention[22] but are savvy enough to realize their friends are not necessarily reliable sources of sexual health information. Boys are also acutely aware that peer influence is not always positive.

The Ayala study asked a focus group of university-aged men to look back on their experiences in adolescence. They talked about the pressure boys can put on other boys to prove their masculinity through sexual experience:

> "It's just so much pressure…to, you know, keep up with the rest of them, that you don't really care what you're dealing with or how you do it [sex], as long as you do it."

A few men in the study talked about how this pressure led them do whatever was needed to "get the job done" without regard for the risks of disease or even their own personal feelings or desires.[23] After all, a real man never says "no" to sex, right?

And herein lies the problem for teenage boys: they are armed with the "culturally ascribed authority to orchestrate sexual encounters" [24] but lack the facts they need to ensure these encounters are safe and healthy. Friends are less than reliable. Adults are either oblivious to the needs of boys or too nervous to discuss their emerging sexuality. Media are often the only option for sexually curious boys, but as an educational resource, most are suspect, dominated as they are by depictions of casual hookups and "sex as masculinity" messaging.

Hookup Culture and Unsafe Sex

When I was in my teens, hooking up with someone meant getting together to hang out. The meaning of the term is no longer so innocent. There is no single definition of a "hookup" but most people take it to mean a sexual encounter outside of a committed relationship, involving anything from kissing to oral, anal, or vaginal sex. Some experts consider a hookup a one-time thing, akin to a one-night stand, while others say that multiple encounters with the same person still count as hookups.[25]

Many a newspaper article has discussed the rise of hookup culture, based, as it is, on casual sex between young adults. Depending on what you read, the hookup trend might be a sign that civilization is ending or a liberating and empowering experience, especially for women.[26] (The key word being "women" since no one would be so blasé about casual sex between boys and girls.) Moral judgments aside, there is concern about the filtering down of hookup culture to teens and the physical and emotional consequences of the promiscuity it encourages.

Hookup culture is the new normal in the media aimed at teen and young adult audiences. Reality shows like *The Real World*, *Below Deck*, *Party Down South*, and *Slednecks* are based almost exclusively on drinking and bed-hopping. In fact, television in general shows a fair amount of casual sex. In a study of programming from 2004-2005 on broadcast and cable networks, communications professors Keren Eyal and Keli Finnerty zeroed in on depictions of sexual intercourse and found an even divide between casual and committed sexual relationships. According to their content analysis, 32% of intercourse depictions occurred between partners with no previous sexual relationship and 14% between couples who had just met. In comparison, 29% took place between couples with an established non-married relationship, and 15% between married couples. And while most occur between adults over the age of 25, Eyal and Finnerty found that 16% of portrayals of intercourse involved teens and young adults.[27]

Popular films also emphasize sex among strangers. In a content analysis of the top 200 films released worldwide between 1983 and 2003, pediatrician Hasantha Gunasekera found that 70% of scenes depicting sexual intercourse were between new partners.[28] Print media also contribute to the trend. Lad magazines, in particular, focus on promiscuity with sexual fantasies like anal, oral, group, and public sex with strangers depicted as highly desirable or even rites of passage for men.

With all this casual sex to influence them, it seems logical to assume that teens are having more sex than in years past, but that is not actually the case.

Since 1991 the American Centers for Disease Control (CDC) has tracked the number of high school students (boys and girls) who have ever had sexual intercourse. The numbers decreased from 54.1% to 46.8% between 1991 and 2013.[29]

In Canada, the numbers of teens having had sex has stayed roughly the same over a similar time period, with 32% of 15-17-year-olds reporting having had intercourse in 1996-97 and 30% making the same claim in 2009-10.[30]

Intercourse is not the only type of sexual activity, of course. Media reports have sounded the alarm about an increase in oral sex among teens. A variety of studies about the prevalence of oral sex have been done, some focusing on a boy's entire sexual history and some isolating a single year of a boy's life. In Canada for the year 2002-2003, 32% of boys in grade nine reported ever having oral sex, a number that increases to 53% for grade eleven boys. The numbers for both age groups represent an increase of 4% over a ten-year period. In the US, the numbers are broken down by giving and receiving: in 1995, among never-married males aged 15-19, 39% had ever given oral sex and 49% had ever received. Unlike in Canada, the numbers in the US decreased to 34% and 46%, respectively, in a study covering the years 2006-2010. [31]

Anal sex is also thought to be more prevalent among young people now than in the past. Historical numbers are hard to come by but the CDC has some comparative data showing no increase between 2002 and the years 2007-2010. In each report 11% of boys aged 15-19 reported having anal sex with an opposite-sex partner. For the record, the numbers are considerably higher among men aged 20-24, with 32.6% reporting anal sex in 2002 and 35.3% in 2007-2010. It appears, then, that anal sex is far more common among adults than teens. [32, 33]

With no real increase in the number of teens having sex, parents might wonder if there is reason to worry about hookup culture. The short answer is "yes." Hookup culture may not entice kids to start having sex but it does promote unsafe behaviour to those who are already doing it.

Much has been written about the psychological impacts of hookups—guilt, regret, shame, and lowered self-esteem, all of which are felt more intently by females than males—but there are also physical consequences, namely STI transmission.

Condoms are the main barrier against the spread of infection but the very nature of hookups mitigates against consistent condom use. Because hookups are typically unplanned, the people involved may not have condoms or may, in the heat of the moment, decide not to use them, especially in cases of oral or anal sex. Communication is also an issue in hookups since the people involved are not in a relationship and may not feel comfortable discussing condoms. The promiscuity inherent in hookup culture is another potential problem. As we all know, a higher number of sexual partners means an increased chance of encountering and spreading an STI.[34]

Alcohol is another issue. Although they were speaking of college students, professor of politics Caroline Heldman and sociologist Lisa Wade wrote in 2010 that "[a]lcohol use, if not drunkenness, is a central part of hook-up culture."[35] While certainly more prevalent among college students, alcohol and drugs are a factor for some high school students too: 26% of sexually active high school boys in the CDC survey reported using alcohol or drugs before their last sexual intercourse, including 27.6% of those in grade 9.

Despite the potential for negative consequences, many media emphasize the fun and excitement of casual sexual hookups. Television in particular tends toward a rather simplistic view of the impact of sexual relationships. Most characters experience only emotional outcomes—primarily happiness—rather than the complex mix of positive and negative emotional, social, and physical consequences that greet teens in the real world.[36]

Eyal and Finnerty note that this emphasis on emotional outcomes means physical consequences like STIs are largely ignored on television. Communications scholars Susannah Stern and Jane D. Brown made note of a similar issue in the films aimed at teens: "…the consequences of sexual behavior have been underrepresented when compared with reality. Sexually transmitted diseases, in particular, are nearly invisible in films featuring teen sexuality despite an ongoing epidemic among adolescents."[37]

Epidemic is a pretty strong word but as we will see in the next section, STI rates are increasing among teens and condom use is not keeping pace. Communications professor Kirstie M. Farrar offers one reason:

> …one of the main barriers to emerging adults engaging in safer sexual behavior is the lack of a complete sexual script specifying how to have these conversations with one's partner…Young people are not likely to get these scripts from school or their parents or…from most media portrayals.[38]

One look at the television dial makes clear just how rare such safe sex scripts are. The reality shows I named earlier—MTV's *The Real World* franchise, *Slednecks*, and its nearly identical precursor *Buckwild*—all show excessive alcohol use and repeated hookups between friends with nary a condom in sight. With their emphasis on casual sex, these programs seem ideally suited to messages about consequences but there were none to be found in the episodes I watched; a missed opportunity given that these shows feature real people who could, theoretically, demonstrate real reactions to sexual situations.

The problem is not limited to so-called unscripted programs, although they seem to be the worst offenders. Before the wave of party-down, partner-swapping reality shows we know today, the Kaiser Family Foundation published its fourth *Sex on TV* report. Released in 2005, the report noted that TV programs popular with teens have a greater number of sexual scenes than the industry norm, yet only 5% of scenes with sexual content mention any risk or responsibility topics (R/R) like sexual precaution (efforts to prevent sexually transmitted infections and pregnancy), negative consequences, and sexual patience (waiting until a relationship matures and both partners are equally ready to have sex).

The report notes that the percentage of R/R messages is higher in teen programs than others, but 5% is still not a great ratio. Nor does the situation seem to be improving: the number of R/R messages had not changed between the Foundation's 2005 report and the 2002 version.

Researchers believe the absence of risk and responsibility messages may be a contributing factor in the high STI rates seen among adolescents and young adults.[39]

Certainly, media have no obligation to provide safe sex messages, but it wouldn't hurt if they did. In fact, it might even help. Studies have shown that media can have a positive impact on rates of condom use. A report done in 2003 when the television show *Friends* was popular showed that after watching an episode centred on a pregnancy resulting from condom failure, 65% of viewers recalled the condom failing and 10% talked with an adult about condom use.[40]

In her 2006 study, Farrar surveyed university-aged women who watched television dramas with scenes of intercourse emphasizing condom use. These young women had significantly more positive attitudes about condoms and safe sex than women who watched comparable scenes of intercourse with no mention of condoms. The men in the study were unaffected but Farrar found enough evidence to conclude that people's attitudes about sexual topics can be "influenced in a positive way by responsible sexual portrayals on television."[41] She believes that helping people feel more positive about condoms will lead them to initiate conversations about condom use with their partners.

As the *Friends* and Farrar studies show, sexual messages on popular television programs resonate with teens. Constant sermonizing about safe sex would likely cause them to tune out but subtle and clever plotlines with safe sex undertones could help create new sexual scripts for teens to follow.

For now, however, messages about safe and responsible sex are virtually nonexistent in our popular culture. Considering adults' spotty record on sexual education and boys' use of media to fill in the gaps in their sexual knowledge, this is a worrisome situation.

Sociologist Marshall Smith talks about the disparity between sexual education and the media reality that kids face: "…adolescent sexual discussion has been restricted in formal sexual education and in religious and family settings. On the other hand, adolescents encounter an increasingly sexualized media environment, including the glut of sexual content online. These historical circumstances are unique."[42]

Indeed they are, and the misinformation spawned by these unique circumstances has left many teen boys ignorant of the risks of disease from "non-coital" sexual contact (oral and anal) and the importance of using condoms correctly and consistently.

Condoms, STIs, and Pregnancy

A comprehensive study published in 2005 noted that oral sex is a potential transmission route for herpes, hepatitis, gonorrhea, chlamydia, syphilis, and HIV. While most teens recognize there is some chance of acquiring an STI from oral sex, 14% believed there was zero chance of contracting HIV or chlamydia from oral sex.[43] (This study did not cover HPV, but there is a risk of acquiring it through oral sex as well.[44,45])

Whether acquired through oral, anal, or vaginal sex, STIs are on the rise among young people. In the US, the Guttmacher Institute notes that although 15- to 24-year-olds make up only one-quarter of the sexually active population, they account for nearly half of the new cases of sexually transmitted infections (STIs) each year. Nearly half of those are human papillomavirus (HPV) infections.[46] There are several strains of HPV and many are harmless, but the so-called high-risk strains (including types 16 and 18) can lead to cervical cancer in women and some rare cancers in men.[47] Among Canadian teens, one of the most recent studies into HPV showed that HPV-16 is the most common STI.[48]

Other STIs are also prevalent in the teen population. In most cases girls are affected in much higher numbers than boys but infections among boys are growing in number:

- Between 2007 and 2011, rates of infection have increased among boys for both chlamydia and syphilis, although the latter is still quite rare.[49,50, 51,52]
- HIV rates are also high among youth. In 2008, people aged 13-24 in the US made up 17% of all people diagnosed with HIV/AIDS,[53] with people aged 20-24 having had the largest percentage of diagnoses (16%) and the highest rate of all age groups (36.9 per 100,000).[54] Canadian statistics for people aged 15-29 show a rate of 26.7% for females and 23.1% for males.[55]
- Gonorrhea is another worry, with the number of infections among American boys aged 15-19 remaining unchanged between 2009 and 2011.[56] In Canada the numbers among boys of the same age rose about 6% between 2005 and 2011.[57]

For young men, the STI problem is especially acute given the general lack of attention they receive from medical professionals regarding their sexual health, and the fact that many STIs are, in males, asymptomatic.[58] If there are no symptoms and doctors are not inquiring about sexual health, boys remain blissfully unaware that they may be spreading disease. The impact of untreated STIs is more pronounced in women, but males can suffer problems like infertility and epididymitis[59] if STIs are left untreated.

Unsurprisingly, inconsistent condom use is the main reason for increases in STI rates. The 2013 CDC study cited earlier found that among high school boys who were sexually active, 34.2% did not use a condom during their last sexual intercourse. Although an improvement over 1991 when 45.5% had not used a condom at last intercourse, the number of non-users is still high.[60]

Arik Marcell also noted problems with condom use. His research showed that while 71% of teen males used a condom at their first and most recent sexual encounter, less than half (48%) reported using a condom with every sexual experience. This number has not changed in over three decades. Parsing these numbers a little more, a 2010 study in *Sexuality Research and Social Policy* noted that any increase in condom use likely applies to sexual intercourse alone and not anal and oral sex, practices done largely without protection and very likely responsible for some of the uptick in STIs.[61]

The lack of condom use is worrying given the promiscuity of some teens. The number of American boys reporting four or more sexual partners in their lifetimes—a gauge of promiscuity—has declined from 23.4% in 1991 but remains at about 17-18%, depending on the study. Even 9% of boys in grade 9 reported having more than 4 sexual partners in their lifetime.[62,63] Canadians may be even more randy. A 2006 report noted that among grade nine males, 22% had had between 4 and 10 intercourse partners, and 7% had had more than 11 partners. [64]

Boys choose not to use condoms for a variety of reasons, including embarrassment when buying them, lack of availability, reduced physical sensation, and issues with planning or discussing condom use with a partner.[65] Some boys also have a fear of looking sexually incompetent; rather than appear inexperienced they may choose to avoid the condom situation altogether.[66]

The Ayala study points to something more fundamental as well: in sexual encounters, boys tend to worry primarily about pregnancy and rarely consider STIs. Across several studies, boys were found to believe that oral contraceptives were all that was needed during intercourse, an indication that STIs are not on their radar. Indeed, among the boys interviewed in the course of Ayala's research, few knew anyone with HIV, a fact that made both HIV and other STIs invisible and intangible to boys.

Media might play a role here too. The Farrar study cited earlier stated that men were not influenced in a positive direction by media depictions of condom use, but one study found that media may influence them in the other direction. Conducted in Switzerland with students aged 16-20, the study found a "statistically significant" association between pornography use and non-condom use, both for males who deliberately sought out porn and those who were exposed to it unintentionally. Swiss youth generally possess a greater degree of sexual health literacy and have higher rates of condom use than North American youth, but, if this study is correct, it appears that even they may mimic the very unsafe practices shown in pornography. The result concerned the researchers because any reduction in condom use could bring with it an increase in STI transmission. Contrary to Ayala, the Swiss researchers hypothesized that the lack of use could stem from the fact that the condom is more often seen as contraceptive rather than a method of preventing STIs.[67]

Yet, even as contraceptives condoms are used far less than they should be, as we saw in the CDC statistics. Even more worrying than the one-third of boys not having used a condom at last intercourse are the 11.5% of teen boys who, in 2013, reported used no contraception whatsoever, a number that had climbed from its low of 9.7% in 2009. [68]

Spotty contraceptive use, whether condoms or other methods, explains why teen pregnancies still occur in the numbers they do. While greatly improved, the number remains as high as 28.2 per 1,000 teens in Canada.[69] By comparison, the rate for girls under the age of 18 in England and Wales was 27.9 per 1,000.[70] The rate in the U.S. is higher still: in 2010 the teen pregnancy rate stood at 57 pregnancies per 1,000 girls, a decline of 15% from the 2008 number but still double that of Canada, England, and Wales.[71] (All three are higher than many countries in Europe, however.)

The risk of pregnancy and STIs is present at any age if a person is not careful, but there is a greater chance of problems when children start having sex at a younger age. Early sexual initiation is more prevalent among some children that others and, contrary to popular belief, media is not always the culprit.

Early Sexual Debut

How early is too early for a child to lose his or her virginity? The statistics cited earlier showed that a significant percentage of boys are sexually active by the time they enter grade 9 and nearly half have had intercourse before they finish high school. Sex in the later teen years is considered normative but sex in the middle-school or early-high-school years is considered early by most clinicians. Sex at that age also brings an increased risk of negative consequences, caused in part by incomplete or late-arriving sex education.

As we've seen throughout this chapter, when it comes to sex, what kids don't know can hurt them, especially if they start having sex at a young age. Younger teens are less likely to use condoms or contraceptives, putting themselves at greater risk of unplanned pregnancies or STIs. Teens who initiate sex at a young age tend to have more sexual partners over the course of their lifetime, resulting in a higher probability of acquiring an STI. They also tend toward more reckless sexual behaviour, increasing their STI risk as they get older. [72,73] And, like older teens, few younger teens are aware the STI risk presented by oral sex and believe it is a safe alternative to vaginal sex.[74]

So what leads children to become sexually active at an early age? Adults may be concerned that sexual portrayals in media encourage youth to start having sex, but there are other, more important factors involved.

- Psychiatrist Argyro Caminis noted that sexual intercourse may be an indicator of psychological distress when it occurs before the age of 15. That is, sexual activity may be a symptom of other problems like depression, anxiety, and substance abuse.
- A Dutch study concurred with Caminis, noting that "high levels of rule-breaking and aggression" were associated with a higher likelihood of early sexual debut among males. This study also found a link between low levels of maternal attachment and early initiation.[75]
- Lower socioeconomic status (SES) may also be a factor in early sexual initiation, since economic stress and constantly working parents can lead to reduced parental monitoring.[76]

A study by psychologists Myeshia N. Price and Janet Shibley Hyde found that the amount of time spent watching television was a significant factor in early sexual debut, but not the only one. They concluded that the cumulative effect of multiple factors—poor parental relationships, advanced pubertal development, low self-esteem, and higher rates of externalizing behaviours like ADHD— puts boys at risk of early sexual initiation. The more risk factors a boy has, the greater the likelihood of early sexual debut. For example, a boy who watches a lot of sexual content on TV and has low self-esteem and a poor relationship with his parents has a much higher chance of becoming sexually active at a young age than someone who has none or only one of those risk factors. On the flip side, the conclusions from this study indicate the importance of parents: kids who watch a lot of sexual content but have a good relationship with their parents or no other risk factors are more likely to delay having sex.[77]

The research summary I have offered here just scratches the surface, but it seems that sexualized media is not a primary factor in the age of boys' sexual debut. The decision to initiate sex is a complex one and not just a matter of seeing people do it on-screen. Parental involvement and the psychological health of a boy play a far larger role than media in determining when a boy will start having sex.

One factor that few people consider as motivation for a boy's sexual debut, however, is love. Affection for a girl might not lead a boy to have sex at an early age but it is often the reason he has sex for the first time.

What's Love Got to Do With It? Masculinity Norms and Boys' Relationships

One of the greatest myths about adolescent male sexuality is that boys are always seeking sex and never love. While not an issue of physical health, this misconception can affect boys' emotional health and it is one of which parents and boys themselves need to be aware.

Boys want intimacy and love in their romantic relationships more than most people realize but cannot typically give voice to these desires. When you consider prevailing cultural norms about manhood and masculinity, it is easy to understand why. Psychologist Ronald F. Levant defined our culture's highly restrictive view of manhood as including: "the requirement to avoid all things feminine; the injunction to restrict one's emotional life; the emphasis on achieving status above all else; the injunction to be completely self-reliant; [and] the emphasis on toughness and aggression…"[78]

While Levant was talking in general terms about masculinity norms, each element of his definition applies to boys' romantic lives. Emotional expression, considered a highly feminine behaviour, is verboten. In the romantic realm, status—ever important for boys—is demonstrated through sexual prowess and conquests, not committed relationships. Self-reliance means never having to depend on a girl or allowing her take up too much space in a boy's life. Toughness means not succumbing to "wussy" feelings like love.

Taken together, the complete stereotype is summed up in an article by sociologist Peggy Giordano and colleagues: many boys, incited by their peers, view the heterosexual world not as a place for romance but "as another arena in which they can compete and score."[79] Or, at least, that is the impression they try to create as they negotiate the often thorny terrain of adolescent sex and relationships.

For a lot of boys this posturing is just a façade. The Giordano report found that most boys do not fit the stereotype of conquest-seeking Lotharios. In fact, boys in her study showed low levels of confidence in their relationships, insecurity about their level of sexual and relationship experience, and feelings of love equal to those experienced by girls.

Pediatrician Mary Ott discovered how deep those feelings run. In a 2010 report, she cites research indicating that ninth grade boys ranked intimacy as an important relationship goal, above sexual pleasure and social status.[80] Canadian statistics reinforce this point. A 2006 study showed that males are less motivated by "love" than females but among boys in grades 9 and 11 "love for the person" is cited as the most common motivation for their first experience of sexual intercourse.[81]

So why does swagger rule?

Media depictions of male sexuality are one reason, but the real pressure to adhere to social norms seems to come from boys' peers. Ott noted the tension many boys feel between their actual relationship goals and the need to demonstrate their masculinity, particularly in group situations where boys may feel the need to play the part of "stud." Giordano and colleagues also saw evidence of this type of pressure, noting that the boys they talked to had a fear of being seen as "controlled" by their girlfriends. This fear even led some boys to denigrate their girlfriends when hanging out with their male friends.[82]

All told, there can be considerable stress on boys who feel pulled in two directions: compelled to act the part of the guy's guy with their friends while simultaneously seeking more intimacy with their girlfriend.

For boys who have taken the bold step into a committed relationship, things aren't necessarily easy either. Even those who truly wish to express their feelings or desires may not know how. Boys in the Giordano study reported "significantly higher" levels of awkwardness in their communication than girls. Tristan Abbott, a facilitator in Calgary's WiseGuyz sexual education program, noted in *The Walrus* article that he has seen many boys fumble in simply expressing feelings. One reason is that, unlike girls, they are not encouraged to practice loving talk. As a result, "[s]ome have almost no emotional vocabulary, beyond sad or mad or happy…There's not a lot of nuance."[83]

There is another area where boys' shaky communication skills are failing them: the act of asking for and ensuring consent, a vital skill rarely taught or even discussed with young people.

Chapter 4—No Means No, or Does It? Cultural Confusion Over Consent

> "The notion of actively seeking consent is largely alien to young people, and compounded by information from adults that focuses on the importance of 'giving' rather than 'getting' consent."
>
> *Maddy Coy et al*[1]

The topic of consent made regular headlines in 2014, particularly on university campuses in the United States, Canada, and the UK, when female victims of rape went public about the underwhelming administrative and police response to the crimes committed against them. In one case from Oxford University, a female student going by the pseudonym of Maria Marcello talked about being raped in her dorm room by a man she had just met while passed out drunk. She had DNA evidence linking the man to the crime but was told by police to drop the charges because it would be her word against his and, therefore, too hard to prove.[2]

The crime committed against Marcello falls under the category of acquaintance rape, a close kin of date rape. But rape is not the only type of violation to occur on university campuses or in other places young men and women meet. The *Guardian* article that described Marcello's case detailed other instances when lines were crossed: women being groped, having hands put up their skirts, being touched in a sexual manner in a crowded bar, and being photographed while sleeping by male students who later posted the pictures online. While the females affected by these crimes were horrified, the men who committed the offences had very different reactions: some laughed and others blithely dismissed the women's protests and concerns.

The common element in all of these cases is a lack of consent. Whether out of wilful disregard for these women's bodies or genuine ignorance about when consent is needed, it is clear that none of the men sought or received consent for their actions. As the examples above show, consent is not just relevant in intimate encounters. It also applies to unwanted touching, leering, catcalling, or any situation where boundaries are not respected and people are made to feel uncomfortable or unsafe. Nor is consent strictly a male-versus-female issue; boys and men must also deal with unwanted advances.

Because it is rarely modelled in our culture or discussed at school or in the home, consent is a murky proposition for young people. Yet it is critical that they understand consent, especially as they approach their teenage years and become sexually curious and, in many cases, sexually active.

Gender Codes and the Communication of Consent

Despite the importance of sexual consent, there has been very little research into young people's understanding of it. Psychologist Terry Humphreys is one of the few researchers who have studied the subject. Working primarily with university-aged men and women, he found that most students understood the "ingredients that ideally make up a consensual sexual encounter" but found the "practical application" of these ideas considerably more complicated.[3] In other words, what happens in the heat of the moment trumps all rational thinking about consent.

Humphreys' findings were echoed in a 2013 study of youth aged 13-20 by Maddy Coy and colleagues at London Metropolitan University. The Coy study went one step further, pinpointing the reasons consent gets lost in the haze of sexual desire: "…young people's understandings of consent in the abstract are relatively clear, but when applied to real situations, gendered codes of behaviour and victim blame change how they make sense of sexual negotiation."

These gendered codes can be seen in the lessons taught by the heterosexual script: boys have uncontrollable sexual urges and must seek to satisfy them; girls cannot be overtly sexual and are responsible for setting limits on sexual relationships. This script, the stereotypes within it, and the social implications that emerge from it can affect the sexual decision-making of both boys and girls.

For boys, sexual experience brings status or, according to the Coy study, "man points." Each sexual conquest means "points" that translate to higher standing in a peer group and definitive proof of a boy's masculinity. In the context of consent, boys who want to maintain their status may push harder for sex or disregard a girl's requests to stop.

Young women, conditioned to believe they should be "good girls," face considerable conflict in sexual relationships. One the one hand, a girl may fear being called a "slut" or "whore" for going too far even if it is what she wants. On the other hand, if she tries to stop a boy after he gets started, she will be blamed for leading him on and labelled a "tease." The pressures of these labels weigh on a girl at the very moment she must decide whether to go for broke or put on the brakes in a sexual encounter and can affect her choice.

The question in all sexual encounters, for both boys and girls, is this: are they genuinely consenting if they base their decisions on what is expected of them rather than what they really want? They are not being forced by their partner but may feel forced by the social norms that govern sexual relationships. There is potential social fallout in all directions: boys who do not succeed with a girl or choose to be patient will be considered less manly; girls who go too far will be demeaned; and girls who fulfill their role as sexual gatekeeper will be blamed for tempting a boy then leaving him cold. These kinds of pressures are important for parents and educators to understand so they can, in Coy's words, help kids make better sense of sexual negotiation.

The Coy study also talks about the way teens frame consent and the inherent problems with prevailing definitions of the term. Young people consider consent something to be given rather than gotten, with agreement to have sex "read in terms of absence of resistance." In short, kids don't ask for a yes; they wait until they are told no.[4]

And how do young people, in the midst of a very intense moment, communicate consent? The short answer is that they do not, at least not verbally. As Humphreys found, women state a preference for explicit consent but engage in passive, non-verbal assent to sex—not resisting or saying no, letting things progress to intercourse, responding to a man's advances—or "no response signals" which include saying nothing, doing nothing, and believing their consent was obvious. Humphreys found that as intercourse became a real possibility verbal consent was more likely to be given, but 65% of the students he surveyed found the verbal "ask" for consent very awkward.[5]

For the teens in Coy's study, non-verbal cues were also assumed to indicate consent: reciprocation of kissing and taking off clothes meant a definite "yes" even though it was not expressed clearly.

Some boys use non-verbal cues of their own. Professor of Health Promotion Kristen Jozkowski talks about the "borderline pressure" some boys and men apply as a means of seeking consent: taking a girl to a private place, closing the door, continuing with the activity until she stops him.[6] The onus, then, is on her to say "no," not on him to ask for a "yes," proof again that consent is something given, not gotten.

The problem with any kind of non-verbal cue is that it can be misinterpreted. Sex role stereotypes play a part in this lack of understanding. Teens often interpret signals through what they think is appropriate for each gender.[7] Mild reluctance on the part of a girl may be seen as "token resistance," or her playing the part of "good girl." As a result, a boy may ignore her protests if he believes she is just being coy. On the other hand, a girl who has let things progress might succumb to a boy's "borderline pressure," believing that he cannot control himself and she is responsible for letting things get out of hand.

Non-verbal cues are especially suspect when certain situational pressures[8] intrude and prevent a person from acting in accordance with his or her true desires. Among adolescents and young adults, the primary intervening factors are alcohol and drugs. Both substances can loosen inhibitions and cause people to consent when under the influence or, in a worst-case scenario, lose the capacity to say no.

Unfortunately, as we saw in the previous chapter, media does its share in telling kids that drunken sex is fun. The use of alcohol is a common theme in reality shows. A scene from the MTV program *Are You the One* is typical of the reality genre. In this instance, a man and woman are interviewed about their tryst. They are questioned separately, and she indicates the hookup happened only because they were drunk.[9] Programs like *The Real*

World and *Below Deck* also trade on the idea that excessive alcohol consumption is fun, regardless of where it might lead.

Alcohol figures in stories in lad magazines as well, a trend noted by political scientist Nicole Krassas and colleagues, who found a recurring theme of "intoxication makes sexual conquest better" in these publications.[10] I noticed and was troubled by the frequency of the latter theme in an article I read on the website of lad mag *FHM*, given the association between alcohol and date rape. Entitled "FHM's best ever Ladies' confessions: the top 100," the article included 22 stories where women got drunk or drank heavily. There were no crimes committed or even implied, but the subtext in many stories was that women who drink heavily want sex badly and are always ready, willing and able, with an emphasis on the word "willing," which is not always the case in the real world.[11]

A Lack of Clarity on Consent

To avoid confusion and keep safe from unwanted sex, kids need strategies and clarity about consent. So, who's providing that clarity? Again, the research is spotty, but neither parents nor schools have proven a reliable source of information on the topic of consent. Although many teens might prefer parents as a resource, the Coy study showed that most find it awkward to talk to Mom and Dad about sex and consent. As we saw in the previous chapter, most boys view school-based sex education as inadequate, especially on the topic of healthy relationships.[12] A study of boys in Toronto by Planned Parenthood showed that healthy relationships topped the list of issues they want to learn more about[13] but it is not something they often hear discussed at school. UK-based Coy and colleagues interviewed students an ocean away from Toronto, but found similar attitudes about sex ed: school does not talk about "anything that actually matters in real life situations."

Like Ayala in the previous chapter, Coy asked teens where they learned how to behave in sexual relationships. The majority indicated that media plays a big part. Sources cited include:

- magazines with sex tips and "real life dilemmas;"
- TV programs, including soap operas featuring young people;

- the Internet, which is code for "pornography."

Like others who have researched adolescent use of pornography, Coy found that most boys who watched X-rated films online admitted that they did so in part to learn about sex and, by extension, consent.[14] And we all know how accurate pornography is about sexual relationships. Consent is non-existent in these films. Men can do just about anything they want without a peep of protest from a woman. Porn is an extreme environment, but its depictions of consent are not far off the mainstream. In pop music, television, film, and music videos consent is glossed over or ignored completely.

Consider the 2014 hit song *Blurred Lines*, widely condemned for promoting the idea that men can assume consent with no need to ask. The video only made matters worse. The sight of several naked young women cavorting around fully-clothed men singing "I know you want it" fairly screamed of male sexual entitlement.

Popular television program *Supernatural* has also shown questionable judgment on the topic of consent. A group of fans even started a petition on Change.org asking the show's creators to stop creating scenes of sexual violence and "dubious consent."[15] Several episodes are cited in the petition, including one in which lead character Dean talks about killing a woman but tells another man he would have given him "an hour with her first." No mention is made of what the woman might have wanted.[16] An episode from season 9 included a scene where it was implied that a young soldier enjoying his first weekend pass into town could have his way with a woman if he plied her with alcohol: "So I set it all up. Jamie's waiting at the bar and has a thing for men in uniform. So, just start buying shots, and you can thank me in the morning."[17]

Speaking of dubious consent, in another season 9 episode, Dean preys on a woman knowing that she, as the chastity counsellor at a local church, has vowed not to engage in sex. He manipulates her by feigning an interest in celibacy, insists on walking her home, lights a candle when he arrives—all the better to seduce her—and ogles her while she prays. The entire scene is brimming over with implications about his entitlement to sex: she removes a baggy sweatshirt and spends the rest of the scene in a skin-tight, somewhat sheer tank top that shows a too-small bra; when she bends down to reach some books her tiny top rides up and shows more skin. She eventually and unambiguously consents to sex, but the entire setup smacks of "no means yes" messaging. It is clear she is struggling with her newfound commitment to celibacy yet he lies to her to get her alone, refuses to back down, and gets his way in the end.[18] All in all, some pretty poor lessons for young viewers.

The issue of consent does not just affect female characters on *Supernatural*. In this series, possession by demons, angels, and reapers is the norm, so consent becomes rather confused for all characters. In a 2013 episode entitled *I'm No Angel*, a woman named April initiates sex with male character and former angel Castiel, who finds out later that she is not who he thought she was. Her body had been inhabited by a reaper sent to kill Castiel. In a statement fraught with sexual imagery, the reaper clarified that April "didn't mind [him] entering her one bit." It is unclear whether this statement is proof that she consented to being "entered" or if the act was carried out by force.

This episode was roundly criticized by fan bloggers for its overtones of non-consensual sex in which both Castiel and April were victims: he believed he was engaging in sex with a woman he was attracted to, while she had her body taken over and used for sex. As the Change.org petition and other fan bloggers noted, April could not consent to this use of her body and Castiel's uninformed consent could not possibly be construed as real consent. The situation in this story is bizarre, what with the possessions of other bodies, but the concerns about consent are real. Castiel was not aware of what was really going on and despite the way it was presented, the kind of manipulation he endured is not a valid way of attaining consent.

Even cultural depictions of loving, gentle sex lack basic references to consent. In the vast majority of cases on television and in film, sex just happens with little or no discussion. In non-explicit fictional portrayals like those found in the soapy dramas favoured by teens, sex is an act of passion. Characters get caught up in the moment and things progress with little or no hesitation. Few characters take the time to ask permission.

Comedies can get in on the act too. Sitcom *The Mindy Project* covered the issue of consent with questionable results in a 2014 episode entitled *I*

Slipped. The "I" was Mindy's boyfriend Danny who "slipped" his penis into a place Mindy did not want it. Danny pretended it was an accident but then later admitted he made the move on purpose because "sometimes a guy just has to try something." Mindy cheerily forgave him but didn't stop there. Desperate to please him and worried that he found her boring, she invited him to do what he wanted after sedating herself to numb the discomfort she felt for anal sex. Lessons were learned and the episode ended with Mindy very politely asking Danny to "run it by her first" when he had the urge to do something "freaky." Danny then suggested sex in a hospital bed—Mindy having been admitted after mixing her sedatives with scotch and passing out. When Mindy declined he joked that "asking sucks."[19]

What is the takeaway from this episode for any young man who happened to tune in with his family? A reinforcement of stereotyped sexual roles with a healthy degree of ambiguity about consent: the man is initially portrayed as the sexually adventurous one; the woman fears being too prudish; he tries something invasive without asking first; and she gives into his request despite not really wanting to. The fact the episode tackled consent is positive, but its end result is less so.

Unsurprisingly, the reality genre is particularly bad when it comes to depicting consent. As we saw earlier, many of these programs are based on promiscuity and hookups with consent rarely, if ever, mentioned. As I noted in the previous chapter, reality shows are the perfect forum for responsible talk about sex but such messaging seems to be anathema to producers.

A demonstration of consent would not have to be a scene stealer or mood killer. A simple "Are you okay with this" between kisses would go a long way. Yet such examples are few and far between in the media popular with teens. The end result? Not asking is seen as normal.

These examples prove the truth of a statement from Terry Humphreys, who wrote that media are saturated in sexual imagery but tell us "little about how to negotiate our daily sex lives with partners whose reactions actually matter to us."[20] He concludes that young people need more "concrete examples of successful behavioral strategies for negotiating sexual consent,"[21] especially since so many get cues from the popular culture that surrounds them.

Boys need these lessons not just so they can understand a girl's attempts to say no, but also so they can feel free to say no themselves. Stereotypes that position boys as sexually insatiable and tie masculinity to sexual experience can exert pressure on boys to perform even when they may not want to. As journalist Rachel Giese noted in *The Walrus* article cited in the previous chapter, boys are repeatedly told in sexual education classes that "no means no," but they are rarely asked if they would like to say no themselves.[22]

Changing Attitudes

In North America, governments are making an effort to talk about consent, especially as it pertains to men and boys. US Vice-President Joe Biden has been involved in the creation of public service announcements (PSAs) involving several high-profile celebrities. The first, called *1 is 2 Many*, featured male actors like Daniel Craig, Benicio del Toro, and Steve Carell along with President Barack Obama, and emphasized the need for clear consent. The second, called *It's On Us*, included male and female actors in a more wide-ranging message about being proactive in preventing sexual assault and not blaming the victim.[23,24]

Specific states have gone even further, challenging the prevailing notion that the absence of resistance in a sexual situation means consent. In response to high numbers of sexual assaults on college campuses, the state of California adopted requirements for colleges that receive state money to follow when investigating such crimes. Dubbed "yes means yes," the law defines consent as "an affirmative, conscious and voluntary agreement to engage in sexual activity" and clearly states that lack of resistance and silence do not constitute consent. It also states that someone who is drunk, drugged, or unconscious cannot grant consent.[25] The influence of the law is spreading. Shortly after its passage in California, New York governor Andrew Cuomo ordered a similar approach for all campuses of the State University of New York, with plans to expand the law to all colleges and universities.[26] The laws have their critics but have certainly drawn attention to the need for clear consent in sexual relationships. Still, there are people for whom the concept of consent remains unclear, including younger teens.

Coy's research found that teens aged 13-14 are less likely to recognize nonconsent than older boys and girls. Will they be influenced by news stories about "yes means yes" policies on college campuses in the US? Not necessarily. Other points of confusion with consent also emerge among adolescents. For example, if a couple is in a relationship where intercourse has occurred before, is consent necessary each time they have sex? Is it necessary to ask for consent at each step of a sexual encounter, from kissing to sexual touching and all the way to actual intercourse?

These are the kinds of questions younger teens have, yet, as we have seen, few receive answers from parents, school, or media. There are also issues with the single-gender focus of most sexual consent initiatives. Girls can also take things too far so it important to communicate to teens that people of both sexes must seek consent before engaging in sexual behaviour.

For some children, the situation may slowly be changing. Schools in some jurisdictions in Canada are seeking to provide younger students with much-needed information about consent. In 2015, the province of Ontario began implementation of a new sexual education curriculum that would introduce the general concept of consent in grade 2. The intent at that age would be to teach lessons about respecting boundaries and listening to the word "no." Age-appropriate lessons in consent would continue throughout elementary school.[27] The changes in Ontario motivated school boards in other provinces to push for the inclusion of consent in their own curricula, including Alberta and British Columbia.[28,29]

As these Canadian educators realize, the earlier discussions about consent start, the better. Without clear lessons on consent from a young age, boys are left to figure things out for themselves. In a media environment lacking positive examples of consent, the end result is blurred lines that can all too easily be crossed.

Chapter 5— When Things Go Too Far: Sexual Aggression, Harassment, and Assault

> "This is the essence of the commercial, male, heterosexual, pornographic imagination: thinking of women as being defined only through their sexuality and that sexuality to be at the service of men's desires." Sut Jhally, *Dreamworlds 3*

Tits, ass, and "legs in high heels."[1] Women are often reduced to these particular body parts in the media adolescent boys see. Comic books and graphic novels, music videos, magazine covers, and commercials for cars, Internet services, beer, and fast food routinely feature barely-dressed women posed to appeal to the male, heterosexual, pornographic imagination described by Sut Jhally. Women are also getting in on the act. The term "self-objectification" is taking on more currency, being used increasingly to describe female celebrities who willingly expose their bodies and overtly sexualize themselves in music videos and Instagram selfies, on stage, and on the red carpet.

This brand of female sexual objectification goes beyond mere titillation. In each objectifying image, women are not only put on display, but also shown to enjoy this treatment, feel flattered by it, and respond to it by preening for more male attention. For these women, sexuality is not about their own wants and desires, but men's: they dress, twerk, grind, pout, and touch themselves primarily to fulfill men's fantasies. In this way, objectification is also tied to the male-as-dominant script I have described in previous chapters: objectified women are reduced to a sexual role and evaluated primarily in terms of how well they can, in Jhally's words, service men's desires.

You may be asking what any of this has to do with sexual aggression. Quite a lot, as we will see. Regular exposure to objectifying imagery can affect the attitudes and actions of boys and men. This is not to say that popular culture will turn boys into rapists, but that stereotyped depictions of male and female sexuality—combined with the lack of strong messages about consent— may instill in boys a distorted view of male and female sexual roles, ultimately influencing their perceptions of how they should act in a sexual relationship, what they should expect from the girls they know, and how hard they should push to get what they want. As communications scholar Stacy Hust said in 2014, "We learn a lot about how to act in a relationship by what we see and read in the media…Bad information can lead to bad decisions."[2]

It must also be said that girls are not the only victims in this environment. Although talked about far less, boys also suffer harassment, sexual assault, and the very serious consequences they bring, often because they do not subscribe to the tenets of the male, heterosexual, pornographic imagination.

The Connection Between Sexualized Media and Aggression

The strong presence of female sexual objectification and male sexual dominance in our media is not surprising when you consider that men are largely in control of the images we see. They are the directors and editors behind most of the sexual imagery in media and they frequently pose women to fulfill stereotypical male fantasies and satisfy the male gaze.[3] Consider a common aesthetic in men's magazine layouts: female models who are wet, barely dressed, and lounging seductively on beds or beaches with full lips partially open and breasts or bottom displayed prominently. Such poses demonstrate the "ritualization of subordination" described by Erving Goffman, showing women as sexually available and often submissive and vulnerable.

Consider also some of the other media aimed at adolescent boys:

- Video games and many graphic novels are notorious for drawing female characters in a highly sexualized manner, like *Fire Emblem: Awakening*, a 2013 game whose website features several female characters in lingerie[4], and anime-inspired comics showing doe-eyed girls in short skirts and tiny tops.

- In the superhero world, female heroes—when present at all—have all aspects of their femininity and sexuality exaggerated, from their bright red lips to their long, flowing hair and buxom figures.
- Professional sports contribute to the problem as well, with jiggling cheerleaders on NFL sidelines and nearly naked models posing seductively in the swimsuit issues of major sports magazines.

Sexual objectification is also common in the films aimed at teen boys. Because the makers of these films do not want to risk a rating higher than PG-13 they keep actual portrayals of sex to a minimum,[5] but there are often implicit messages in these films about gender and the nature of sexual relationships between men and women. For examples we can look to a few popular action films from recent years.

In *Iron Man 3*, a PG-13 film that was released around the time I began writing this book, Iron Man's alter ego Tony Stark talks about "going to town on a woman" and says she will need a cardio doctor after they are done. There is no reference to her role, other than being the recipient of his prowess. His sidekick Happy talks about a "blonde with a big rack" and leers at the nurse tending to him in hospital. There are references to chicks and bimbos, and criminal mastermind Mandarin talks about having two "birds" in his bed, who are later shown playing ping-pong in bikinis for his amusement.[6]

In the film *Transformers: Age of Extinction*, the female lead is regularly shown in revealing clothing with camera angles emphasizing her bottom and legs. An adult male character also refers to this character—a teenage girl—as "hot."[7]

Non-human characters can also objectify women. Common Sense Media reviewed the 2014 film *Teenage Mutant Ninja Turtles* and noted that there were several references to the "sexy body" of female lead April, played by Megan Fox. One of the turtles calls her "hot," says his shell tightens when he sees her (that is, he is aroused), and notes that he has "dibs" on her.[8]

Lad magazines also make female sexual objectification their central focus. Timorous young men may not have the courage to purchase hard copies of these magazines but all of the titles in this genre have robust websites, laden with barely-dressed women, both celebrities and "real girls" who post "sexy selfies" for all the world to see. One of the most egregious sites in recent years was the UK-based *Nuts*. The website included a feature called "Assess My Breasts" that invited young women to upload pictures of their breasts and have them graded by readers,[9] an over-the-top example of women striving to satisfy the male gaze. *Nuts* shut down in 2014, followed by its near-twin *Zoo* in 2015, which had a *Real Girls*[10] photo gallery that allowed readers to rate the images of "regular girls." Popular titles remain in the lad magazine category, including *FHM* and *Maxim*. Also making an appearance in this category is the "new" *Playboy* which seems to have borrowed liberally from the lad magazine model. Like *FHM* and *Maxim*, the new *Playboy* website has a "Girls" menu with access to such edifying articles as "Disney Star Bella Thorne and Her Hot Sisters Lounged Around in Bikinis All Weekend" and "Take Your Top Off Tuesday."[11]

Communications professor Laramie Taylor studied lad magazines and found, unsurprisingly, that all articles were accompanied by sexualized images of women. (A look at the *Maxim* website shows that this trend also extends to the online world.) Taylor believes these images reinforce the idea presented in the text that women are, first and foremost, sexual objects.[12] His point was echoed by political scientist Nicole Krassas and colleagues who noted that the women in lad magazines were routinely objectified and posed as sexually available. The men, on the other hand, had identities outside of the sexual role and were posed in more natural and less sexualized ways.[13]

A similar contrast between men's and women's roles is seen in music videos that show half-dressed women writhing around or simply providing ornamentation for fully-clothed male artists. One of the most egregious examples from recent years was the 2013 hit *Blurred Lines* by Robin Thicke which featured men ogling younger, topless women. More recently, Flo Rida's video for his 2015 song *My House* opened with the singer sitting on a throne while two women in tight, midriff-baring outfits fawned over him. Women's bodies were used routinely as background decoration, employed as lampposts and even for serving food: a woman was shown drinking liquor poured on another woman's body, while in another scene a woman was laid out on a table and used as a sushi platter.[14] The *Billboard* Top 5 song *679* by Fetty Wap showed two women in bikinis soaping up in a bathtub behind a man dressed in jeans and a shirt,[15] while women dressed in lingerie danced in cages in Travis Scott's *Antidote*.[16] Even the video for Drake's hit song *Hotline Bling*, while tame compared to the others described here, included scenes of women in tight lycra clothes and high heels preening seductively while he grooved inside a cubicle in, variously, a parka, hoodie, and oversized sweater.

Female artists follow suit, putting themselves on display in highly sexualized scenes that would, by our cultural standards, look ridiculous if a man were to perform them. Consider if Robin Thicke acted as Miley Cyrus did in her infamous 2013 video for *Wrecking Ball*,[17] seductively licking a mallet or riding naked on a wrecking ball. Place Jay-Z in the Beyoncé role in their video for *Drunk in Love*[18]—he wet and clad in a skimpy bathing suit, crawling all over a fully-clothed Beyoncé who pays him no heed. Or imagine Drake on his hands and knees inside his little box, wiggling his hips as Ariana Grande does in *Focus*, or Fetty Wap writhing on a chair in nothing but a wet t-shirt like Selena Gomez in *Good for You*.[19] These reverse images are shocking to contemplate, but worth considering to realize the position of women in relation to men in much of our sexualized media.

Research into music videos highlights just how common sex role stereotypes and traditional sexual scripts are. In a 2011 paper, psychologist Kathryn Ryan talked about the male stereotypes implicit in many videos and song lyrics: sex defines masculinity, heterosexual men are sexually preoccupied, and men routinely objectify women.[20]

Music can take things much further than basic stereotypes, often veering into degradation and misogyny in both its lyrical and video content.

On two different occasions over a year apart, I consulted the most-watched videos on MTV and the top ten singles lists on the *Billboard* charts and found several songs that included both objectification and degradation. While I do not want to demonize hip-hop and rap, songs in that genre often place at the top of "most watched" video lists and frequently depict sexually insatiable males and objectified females, while also adding a strong undercurrent of misogyny.

The song *Love Me* by Lil Wayne is one example. On March 15, 2013, the song had reached number 9 on the Billboard Hot 100 and number 6 on the MTV Most Viewed list. A guest rap about bitches from fellow musician

Drake opens the song, but further degradation (and explicitness) arrives via Lil Wayne himself who raps: "All she eat is dick/She's on a strict diet/...She say I never wanna make you mad/I just wanna make you proud/I say baby just make me cum, then don't make a sound."[21] Not to be outdone, A$AP Rocky wrote a song called *F**kin Problems* that reached number 8 on the *Billboard* charts in 2013. The song talked about fucking "bitches and broads"[22] and included guest appearances from major artists Drake, Kendrick Lamar, and 2 Chainz. In 2014, 50 Cent noted in his song *Animal Ambition* that that women are gold diggers and he will not give them love or affection since he "just wants some head." [23] In the utterly awful *No Mediocre*, T.I. sinks to new depths with these lyrics:

> All I fuck is bad bitches/I don't want no mediocre/...I never fuck a bitch if she don't do her hair/No more, you won't get no dick if there's a bush down there/Girl I should see nothing but pussy when I look down there/I'm kicked back with four pieces like a Kit Kat/ Me fucking, if you ain't a dime, just forget that.[24]

Researchers have expressed considerable concern over degrading lyrics. Professor of Medicine Brian A. Primack worries that repeated exposure to such lyrics might desensitize individuals to both real-life violence and power differentials related to sex.[25] For their part, psychologist Steven Martino and colleagues believe that degrading lyrics reinforce the male-dominant sexual script depicted in many videos,[26] including those mentioned above which all include the familiar and standard narrative of fully-clothed man surrounded by barely dressed women.

Many of these videos are tagged as explicit but are easily accessible online through the sites teens use to find new music, including Vevo and YouTube. A March 2013 article from *CNN Money* indicates that YouTube's most watched video clips are music videos and the viewers are predominantly teens.[27] Nielsen research backs up this claim, showing that teens "listen" to music through YouTube more than any other source: 64% compared to 56% for radio and 53% for iTunes.[28] Research from YouTube subsidiary Vevo claims that 71% of its users discover new music by browsing and watching music videos online.[29] And the images in videos matter. Unlike music listening, which may be a background activity that does not attract a teen's full attention, watching videos tends to be a primary activity. As a result, the messages may come across more clearly, especially since the visual images are often sexier than the music.[30] Videos can also reinforce the messages in lyrics and clarify ambiguous wording.

Images of male dominance and aggression, female objectification, and degradation are not limited to music videos. Consider a video game being promoted on the main *Hustler* site when I visited it in December of 2012 and still available in 2015. The tagline reads: "Unlike Other Games, in Hustler 3D you don't SAVE the girl…you FUCK her!" The game involves the creation of customized avatars that can be placed in sexual scenes designed by the player. The game must be purchased, which rules it out for most teens, but there are some very graphic images and video clips available for free on the game's website. Screen shots show everything from "basic" sex to bondage (of the woman), a woman being penetrated by a "fucking machine," and several images of a woman with semen on her face and body. In March, 2013, the "What's New" page trumpeted the addition of a "golden shower" option for men that allowed players to "empty the males bladder in arousing or humiliating fashion" (sic) and a rectangular option for the (sex) Toy Editor, so players can "spank those that really deserve it" or "fuck" someone with a brick if they prefer.[31]

The game is designed for men and gives them the chance to create and live out their own sexual fantasies, including many options for humiliating or rough sex. The impact of such imaginary sexual activity is still being studied, but regardless of long-term effects, this type of material is not a healthy introduction to sex for boys who might stumble upon the site: it is violent and greatly exaggerates the traits of the heterosexual script, positioning men as extremely aggressive and even hostile, and women as exceedingly submissive and compliant.

I talked about the imagery in lad magazines earlier, but objectifying and aggressive undertones are also present in the text. I refer to another trend from *FHM*'s 100 stories referenced in the previous chapter. This trend speaks to objectification in a very explicit form and echoes that seen in pornography. Five of the stories featured narratives of the male ejaculating onto the woman, while a further nine stories described the woman gladly and greedily swallowing a man's ejaculate: "…he came in my mouth. I gulped it down." Among these, five stories referenced the "huge loads" ejaculated by the man.[32] As Jackson Katz said in reference to the Steubenville case, such scenes centre on the "complete objectification" of women: "The man—or men—are doing something to her; they are ejaculating into or onto an object rather than having a sexual relationship with another human being."[33]

The fact that these explicit stories are present on the site of a lad magazine troubles some researchers, including psychologists Miranda Horvath and Maddy Coy of the Child & Woman Abuse Studies Unit at London Metropolitan University. In a 2010 article, they refer to lad magazines as "manifestations of the mainstreaming of pornography into the mass media" that promote a "powerful-aggressive" male sexuality."[34]

Because the content of lad magazines is mostly pretty juvenile, many people wonder whether there is any real issue with them. There are two schools of thought: one says these magazines promote a dangerous and misogynistic view of male sexuality and offer a distorted source of sexual information for boys, while the other says they are "ironic" and intended to be humorous.

As a layperson looking at the content of lad magazines and their associated websites, it was difficult for me to find the humour in them. I am not alone in that regard. Researchers have analyzed the content of lad magazines and found that they promote some very negative ideas about sexuality and gender roles.

Beyond the objectification mentioned earlier, one study found some very degrading and disturbing content. In 2012, Horvath and colleagues showed college-aged participants a selection of quotations from lad magazines and convicted rapists. In some cases the source was identified and in others it was not. Participants who were not told the source were asked to guess. Another section of the study asked participants to rate the quotes in terms of their level of degradation.

Overall, men identified more with the quotes when they were attributed to lad magazines, implying that lad magazines may lend a degree of legitimacy to sexist or misogynistic attitudes. The quotes from lad magazines were also rated as more degrading to women than those from the convicted rapists. Finally, participants guessed the source correctly only about 55% of the time, suggesting a strong overlap between rapists' comments and lad magazine content. This ratio came about even though some of the quotes from the lad magazines sounded like advice and could have, theoretically, been more easily identified as coming from a magazine.

Horvath and colleagues note that while many young people might assume there is a boundary between lad magazine content and the statements of rapists—with the former being considered normal and the latter extreme—in reality the distinction is not so clear. The report included a quote from a participant that illustrated how lad magazines could help legitimize negative attitudes toward women. He said that the quotes were "sort of degrading in a way that can be seen to be acceptable if they put it in a glossy magazine." [35]

In case you would like to try the test, here are two sample quotes. See if you can identify which came from a magazine and which from a rapist:

- "You do not want to be caught red-handed…go and smash her on a park bench. That used to be my trick."
- "Some women are domineering, but I think it's more or less the man who should put his foot down. The man is supposed to be the man. If he acts the man, the woman won't be domineering."[36]

As an extreme example of male sexual dominance and aggression in media, I will again mention gonzo porn. In this genre women are blatantly objectified and abused verbally and physically, often by multiple men. These women are also called derogatory names during sex, like cunts, whores, cumdumpsters, and fucktubes.[37] A site called gonzoxxxmovies.com provides many examples of this demeaning and violent sex, including categories like: brutal sex, angry, choking play, "cum in her eyes," and "cum swapping." The category called "triple penetration" included a video called "50 Guys Drill 1 Slut in Every Hole She Has" and others with references to gangbangs.[38]

Given its excessive violence and misogyny, gonzo might not be the genre favoured by younger boys or even most men, but, as *Pornland* author Gail Dines wrote, even outside of gonzo, porn women "are always ready for sex and are enthusiastic to do whatever men want, irrespective of how painful, humiliating, or harmful the act is…what they want always mirrors what the man wants."

What the man wants. That is what it all comes down to. Portrayals of sex in many of the media favoured by many boys are based in a man demonstrating his constant need for sex and his entitlement to get it any way he likes. He, the dominant player, calls the shots and uses her, the sexual object, as he sees fit.

This reduction of women to a sexual role can have a profound impact on boys and young men, creating a fixation on women's sexual activities, linking women's attractiveness to their ability to look and act "hot," and promoting the idea that women are "sexual playthings" who are always eager to fulfill men's wishes.[39]

Sexual objectification can also open the door to aggressive behaviours. In fact, studies have shown links between objectifying and stereotyped media portrayals and various types of sexual aggression:

- regular exposure to stereotyped video game characters is associated with a greater tolerance for sexual harassment and increased rape myth acceptance;[40]
- reading men's magazines, which typically contain objectifying imagery, is linked to lower intentions to seek sexual consent and adhere to sexual consent decisions;[41]
- television portrayals that objectify or degrade women have been shown to play a causal role in gender harassment and sexual coercion intentions.[42]

In short, many of the sexual narratives in teen media reinforce the worst stereotypes about male sexuality and blur the line between what constitutes "normal" guy behaviour and criminal acts. In this grey area many misconceptions about sexual relationships emerge, with rape myths perhaps the most damaging.

She Was Asking For It: Rape Myths and the Bystander Effect

The term "rape myth" refers to the many inaccuracies about sexual assault that permeate our culture. These myths create confusion over what the crime of sexual assault looks like and are one of the reasons that teenage boys who commit sexual assault may fail to see their aggression as anything other than a "normative sexual interaction."[43] Indeed, one survey of American high school students found that 15% of females reported the use of physical force by a male while only 2% of males admitted using physical force, and 14% of females reported being raped while only 1% of males reported committing rape.[44] It seems the boys did not see things the same way girls did, an indication that there is a widespread misunderstanding among teens over what it means to cross the line.

As I started writing this book, an infamous case that shone a spotlight on rape myths was drawing to a close. The rape trial of two teenage football players in Steubenville, Ohio had concluded with guilty verdicts. At the end of the trial there was some fallout, but it didn't land where one would expect. Instead of a thorough public shaming of the perpetrators, they received media sympathy while the victim had to deal with death threats and blaming.

To recap the Steubenville case for those who may not be familiar with it, two high-school football players took full advantage of a girl who was so drunk she could not walk. They penetrated her with their fingers and tried to make her perform oral sex, although she was so far gone she couldn't keep her mouth open. Several people watched. No one intervened. Pictures and video were taken; the most egregious was a clip later released by hacker group Anonymous showing one boy who attended the party laughing and talking about how the girl was "so raped right now."[45] Although the young man who made this comment appears to have understood the nature of the crime committed against this young woman, he may have been the only one. A more typical response came from student Evan Westlake, who said he didn't think that what he was witnessing was rape, "I didn't know exactly what rape was. I always pictured it as forcing yourself on someone."[46] His comment reflects widely held rape myths, a subject explored by psychologist Heather Littleton who has consistently found that people's ideas about rape—their rape scripts—do not match the reality of most rapes. Typical rape scripts are what Westlake had in mind. They involve:

- stranger attack;
- use of severe violence (choking, beating, using a weapon);
- use of rape drugs like Rohypnol (roofies).

In contrast, most rapes:

- are committed by an acquaintance or partner of the victim;
- rarely include severe violence;
- involve the voluntary ingestion of alcohol, leading to impairment.[47]

The experience of most adolescent rape victims reflects the reality described by Littleton but because of scripts that tell them otherwise, most fail to recognize that what happened to them was rape. Teens are typically victimized by an acquaintance, and more often a boyfriend or girlfriend. For teens, drinking is a significant risk factor for sexual assault, and alcohol can also increase the severity of the perpetrator's aggression.[48]

As Littleton notes, a person's rape scripts affect their acceptance of certain rape myths. That is, if people believe rape is a random, extremely violent attack by a stranger, they may think that victims whose experiences vary from that script: are lying; misconstrued "seduction" as an assault;[49] or brought it on themselves because they were drunk or high.

Other rape myths incorporate victim blaming or excuses that exonerate the perpetrator. As professors of social work Sarah McMahon and Lawrence G. Farmer wrote in a 2011 paper, such rape myths have become more subtle over time. Most people no longer overtly state that a girl or woman is to blame for rape but make suggestions that imply she is: she put herself at risk by drinking too much, was too flirtatious, or looked too available in her short skirt. The myth of the overpowering male sex drive is often cited to reduce the accountability of male perpetrators: he was really turned on and couldn't stop himself. Alcohol is also a factor in rape myths, on the one hand blaming victims—she drank too much—and, on the other hand, excusing the aggressor—he was too drunk to know what he was doing or so wasted that he "accidentally" went too far.[50] (Such distortions also exist for male victims of rape, a subject I will address later in this chapter.)

Beyond the act itself, rape myths also affect people's perceptions of what a rapist looks like. There is a notion that men who commit rape are very different from "normal" men. Many people assume that a rapist is sick, psychopathic, sexually frustrated, a drug abuser or alcoholic, or someone who "won't be able to have a woman because he is so gross."[51] In reality, as we have seen, a rapist is far more likely to be a friend or acquaintance of the victim.

Jokes about rape contribute to the problem by minimizing the impact of the crime. In 2013 on the campuses of two Canadian universities, rape chants could be heard during Frosh week. From Saint Mary's University: "SMU boys, we like them young. Y is for your sister. O is for oh so tight. U is for underage. N is for no consent. G is for grab that ass." On the other side of the country at the University of British Columbia, a similar refrain: Y-O-U-N-G at UBC we like em young Y is for yourrr sister O is for ohh so tight U is for under age N is for noo consent G is for goo to jail."[52]

In the world of entertainment, popular television show *Family Guy* has been roundly criticized for its jokes about rape. The show has been on the air for years and some of the problematic episodes are quite old, but that does not make them off-limits for kids. The program is available on Netflix and other online providers, making the entire series available at anytime. As far as rape jokes, a couple of episodes stand out.

In "Movin' Out (Brian's Song)" from season 6, a separate animation scroll featuring Marge Simpson of *The Simpsons* and *Family Guy* character Quagmire appears at the bottom of the screen. He runs up behind her, tackles her and tries to force himself on her while she clearly tries to fend him off. She later escapes but he chases her with his pants halfway down his legs. She returns later to say the sex was fantastic and accepts his invitation for "round 2."[53]

An episode entitled "I Dream of Jesus" includes a scene with lead character Peter asking a waiter in a 50s-themed diner for a record from the jukebox:

> **Peter:** Can I have that record? I love that song. I'll let you have sex with my daughter…
> **Waiter:** I don't know…let's see what your daughter looks like.
> **Peter:** She's…uhh…right there! (The "camera" moves past his actual daughter to an attractive woman wearing a short black dress.)
> **Waiter:** Ok, I'll do her. But can you tell her to cry and beg me to stop?
> **Peter:** I think that can be arranged.[54]

Because *Family Guy* is very popular with adolescent boys it is important to consider what kinds of messages they are receiving about rape when they watch this program: it is not a big deal, can be laughed at, and is not the dark and scary crime some people think it is. If boys add the Marge Simpson clip to the compendium of other images they encounter in our culture, they might start to believe that forced sex is enjoyable for both women and men. That message is certainly clear in pornography where the targets of verbal and physical aggression—primarily women—show pleasure or at least have neutral responses to the behaviours being inflicted on them.[55]

Rape myths also extend to boys who do not commit rape or sexual assault but choose to be bystanders when their peers engage in such crimes. Again, their lack of understanding of what rape means may prevent them from acting, as might an adherence to the "bro code," a term used in the title of a documentary about cultural influences on male attitudes toward women. In this film, Thomas Keith talks about the pressure on boys to keep quiet about the transgressions of their male peers: "Don't snitch, don't tell, don't act, is part of a pervasive male code."[56] The end result is crimes like Steubenville and others like it that, because of the bro code, may never be reported even if witnessed by peers of the perpetrator.

Some studies have shown a link between the bystander effect and the use of pornography. In 2011, John D. Foubert, a university professor who writes regularly about sexual assault prevention, studied the impact of pornography on fraternity men's attitudes about rape. The study focused on three types of pornography: mainstream, rape, and sadomasochistic. Foubert and his research team found that users of all three types of pornography showed significantly less willingness to intervene as a bystander in a rape situation. Those who had watched rape or sadomasochistic pornography also showed much higher acceptance of rape myths than the men who had not watched.[57] I have not yet come across a study that shows whether men's rape myth acceptance is affected by mainstream programming with dismissive attitudes toward rape, like *Family Guy*, but it is a research question worth considering.

The rape myths that prevail in our culture have far-reaching effects. They cause sympathy for the victim to be displaced by blame and distort teens' views of sexual assault, leading them to doubt that actual crimes have been committed. Where there is doubt, there is less effort to step in and more acceptance of the notion that aggressive sex is just a case of guys being guys. The seeds of that doubt are sown in our media and culture, as we saw in my previous discussion of consent and the examples I cited earlier in this chapter: male sexual aggression is glorified; females are presented frequently as sexual objects, barely dressed and submissive; and the use of alcohol is portrayed as fun and a sign of maturity. It is the frat boy mentality writ large, where a predatory male views females as targets and encourages alcohol use to lower inhibitions. If he gets a little out of hand, it is not his fault; she brought it on herself by getting drunk and being flirtatious, and she may even secretly enjoy it.

The same kind of mythology is evident in another type of violation that is less physically invasive but equally traumatizing: sexual harassment.

Harassment and Sexting

Sexual harassment is one of the most common forms of sexual aggression among adolescents. A 2011 report called *Crossing the Line: Sexual Harassment at School* by the American Association of University Women (AAUW) defines sexual harassment as:

> …unwelcome conduct of a sexual nature, which can include unwelcome sexual advances, requests for sexual favors, or other verbal, nonverbal, or physical conduct of a sexual nature. [It] can include conduct such as touching of a sexual nature; making sexual comments, jokes, or gestures; writing graffiti or displaying or distributing sexually explicit drawings, pictures, or written materials; calling students sexually charged names; spreading sexual rumors; rating students on sexual activity or performance; or circulating, showing, or creating e-mails or Web sites of a sexual nature.

The AAUW report notes that teasing of someone who does not conform to gender norms is also sexual harassment, saying that: "Gender harassment is not necessarily sexual in intent or action, but it does address the targeted student's sexuality and is used as a general pejorative to manipulate or control other students."

Male harassment of females stems from the same place as all male sexual aggression, namely the myths that boys: are overwhelmed by sexual desire and can be excused for being assertive or even aggressive about sex (sex role stereotype); have the right to evaluate or criticize girls' sexual appeal (objectification); and are expected to initiate sexual encounters (heterosexual script). These ideas are promoted in our media, as the various music videos, TV programs, and films like *Iron Man 3*, *Transformers: Age of Extinction,* and *Teenage Mutant Ninja Turtles* I discussed earlier demonstrate.

A more recent, troubling example emerged in 2014 via the stalker fantasy video created by Maroon 5 for the band's song *Animals*. In the video, lead singer Adam Levine plays a character obsessed with a woman who has no interest in him. He stands outside her apartment and watches her through her window, takes pictures of her from the street, then later enters her apartment while she is sleeping to photograph her. The video garnered widespread condemnation in popular media for romanticizing sexual violence, a charge that Levine could not have anticipated when, in an interview before the video's release, he referred to it as "really dark and weird and cool."[58] Kids who do not read media criticism might have missed the memo that this video is neither romantic nor cool—it depicts a dangerous obsession and crime.

In school hallways, parties, and other places that young men and women congregate, the behaviours depicted in our media may be reflected in some boys' attitudes and actions. A boy may rub against a girl suggestively in a hallway, tell her she is hot in front of his friends, make sexually suggestive statements, show her sexually explicit images, or call her a slut or "ho" if she is deemed too promiscuous. According to the AAUW study, 56% of girls in grades 7-12 experienced these types of sexual harassment in the single school year from 2010-2011.

The impacts of sexual harassment can be severe. Reactions vary but include: dread of school, absenteeism from school, feeling sick, finding it hard to study, and trouble sleeping. Students who were particularly badly affected noted that they had to find a new route to or from school, quit sports teams or activities, or even change schools.

As the AAUW report and many others have noted, kids' use of electronic devices adds another element to the problem of sexual harassment. Where some would-be harassers may not be bold enough to confront a peer face-to-face, they have fewer inhibitions online. Cyber-harassment includes being sent unwelcome sexual comments, jokes or pictures; being the subject of a sexual joke, rumour, or image posted online; and being called gay or lesbian in a negative way.

Some 36% of girls in the AAUW survey reported being harassed electronically. And those who faced the double whammy of online and in-person harassment—whether male or female—were more likely to be negatively affected than those harassed through only one means.[59]

Sexting is a practice closely associated with cyber-harassment, although its definition is a bit of a moving target. Researchers have questioned whether the practice includes images alone or text as well, and whether it is limited to phone transmissions or encompasses social media. The most common conception of the term centres on user-created content; that is, sexy selfies sent to peers. While the sending of an image is not necessarily a sign of harassment, the coercion that may precede the transmission and the sharing that may follow it definitely constitute harassment. In most cases, it is girls who suffer.

Research shows that sexting is a very gendered activity and is often done under duress. A group of UK teens talked in a 2012 report about how it works. Young men pester young women to send naked or sexual pictures. Girls who do not comply run the risk of being ostracized and ignored by groups of popular boys. Once a boy is in possession of a girl's nude or nearly-nude photo, he may share it without her knowledge or consent to enhance his status among his peers. In the end, he looks cool, but any girl who complains will be blamed for being "stupid enough" to send the photo in the first place.[60] As sociologist Jessica Ringrose and colleagues wrote in 2012, sexting may be a "new" problem but it reflects age-old stereotypes and double standards about male and female sexual roles: boys who collect naked pictures of girls are studs but the girls who send these images are dumb sluts.[61]

As technology evolves, sexting does too. When sexting first emerged it was typically done by phone. It has now moved onto social media with sites like Snapchat which is designed to make "snaps" disappear within ten seconds. Some girls in British Columbia found out the hard way that those pictures can be saved (a fact also acknowledged in Snapchat's support pages). As reported in October, 2014, three teenage boys in Kamloops, BC were charged with criminal harassment after they saved and shared sexual Snapchat images they had coerced from a number of girls aged 13 to 15.[62]

This unauthorized sharing of a peer's sexual images—or exposure, as some teens call it[63]—is yet another example of how objectification and the heterosexual script influence teens' sexual behaviours. In such cases, girls are hassled to put themselves on display in a sexual manner for boys who then share these images, much like boys of an earlier generation would have done with a *Playboy* centrefold. (The key difference being that the *Playboy* model would have consented, an option today's teen girls are not given.) This willingness to exploit girls and leer at them with friends proves the health of a boy's sex drive, an all-important image for teen boys to project to their male peers.

Sexting has garnered many headlines but the jury is out as to its prevalence. Part of the problem is the definition, as I mentioned earlier. With no consistency in the concept of the term, researchers have come up with wildly divergent estimates of the number of teens affected by sexting, with incidence rates ranging from 15% to 40% depending on the study.[64] Even if we accept the lowest estimate, 15% is a significant number of kids. And, as we learned from the tragic story of Amanda Todd, the impact of the harassment that can emerge from a "sext" cannot be underestimated. The British Columbia teenager took her own life after the relentless bullying and sexual extortion she suffered when a single topless photo of her was widely shared.[65]

Of course, male harassment of females is only part of the story. Boys can also be victims of harassment. In the AAUW study, 72% of male harassers said they had harassed a boy, while 50% of female harassers had targeted a male victim. Stereotypes may tell us otherwise, but boys do suffer from the sexual aggression of others. What's worse, they have fewer outlets for sharing their experiences of aggression and the emotional fallout that often follows.

When Boys are Victims

A year after the Steubenville case, another rape story involving football players made headlines. This time the victims were male. In Sayreville, NJ, senior football players subjected first-year players to a hazing ritual that involved, in the carefully chosen words of the media, "improperly touching the boys in a sexual manner." At least one case involved anal penetration with a finger that was later forced into the victim's mouth. Once the story was made public, seven players were charged with sexual assault,[66] undoubtedly because of the outrage expressed in the media.

In our culture, discussions of adolescent sexual aggression typically centre on the familiar notion that boys are the aggressors and girls are the victims. While it is true that girls experience more sexual harassment and assault, the number of male adolescent victims is significant, as is the impact on them.

The fact that few people recognize that males can be victims of assault and harassment shows the degree to which stereotypes and sexual scripts affect people's perceptions of adolescent sexual aggression. Consider the stereotypes of teenage boys: they are emotionally and physically strong, assertive or even aggressive, and perpetually aroused. How could they ever be victims of sexual aggression? If, by chance, they are, wouldn't they just roll with it and laugh it off? How badly could they really be affected?

Quite badly, as it turns out.

The AAUW report cited earlier includes some illuminating statistics about the experiences of middle- and high-school-aged boys:

- 40% of boys in grades 7-12 report being sexually harassed, compared to 56% of girls;
- 22% of boys had experienced unwelcome sexual comments, jokes, or gestures directed at them, compared to 46% of girls;
- 19% of boys had been called "gay" in a negative way, compared to 18% of girls who had had that experience;
- 24% of boys had experienced online sexual harassment, compared to 36% of girls;
- 10% of boys reported being shown sexy or sexual pictures that they did not want to see, compared to 13% of girls.

Even more enlightening is the impact of these behaviours. After being harassed:

- 25% of boys felt bothered to the extent that they did not want to go to school, compared to 37% of girls;
- 21% of boys felt sick to their stomach, compared to 37% of girls;
- 24% of boys found it hard to study, compared to 34% of girls;
- 14% of boys had trouble sleeping, compared to 22% of girls.[67]

Cultural stereotypes would have us believe that boys are largely unaffected by sexual harassment, but these numbers show that is not the case. Boys and girls are both victims and while the numbers are not equal, they are closer than most people probably realize.

For boys, a good amount of the harassment they suffer arises because they do not conform to the traditional male gender role. It is not only boys who are perceived as gay who are affected but also those who are "different;" that is, studious or slower to mature physically.[68]

Both the AAUW report and another done in 2008 by sociologist James Gruber showed that being called "gay" is a particularly damaging form of sexual harassment for boys.[69] As psychologist Leah C. Funk wrote in a 2011 article, "failing to live up to the masculine gender ideal is no laughing matter."[70] It can lead to anxiety and depression, personal distress, lowered sense of school belonging, and lower life satisfaction among boys.[71] This trend is seen also in the research into sexting, which talks about the pressure boys feel to engage in the practice in order to confirm their masculinity or, in another example of the bro code, ignore sexting and harassment by their male peers to avoid being labelled "gay."[72]

Among the findings in the AAUW report, perhaps most surprising is the revelation, cited earlier, that half of the girls who sexually harass their peers choose boys as their targets. The idea of girls harassing boys flies in the face of gender stereotypes and the heterosexual script, which dictates that males are aggressors who act on passive females.

The same kind of misunderstanding exists in cases of sexual assault, which, in the US, are more prevalent among adolescents that any other age group, with one-third of victims falling between the ages of 13 and 17. While the overall numbers of female victims is generally reported as being significantly higher than the number of males, a 2009 study of one group of middle- and high-school-aged teens had some surprising results:

- 28% of middle school boys and 26% of high school boys reported being kissed, hugged, or touched against their will;
- 4.1% of high school boys and 5.5% of girls reported being forced into oral sex, a measure not tracked for middle school students in this study;
- 3.1% of high school boys reported being raped, compared to 11.8% of girls.

In reality, the numbers for sexual assault vary widely between studies, with girls often having much higher incidences of the crime than reported here. One such study pegged the numbers at 15% of boys and 50% of girls. [73] We hear plenty about the female victims of these crimes, and rightly so, but precious little is said about the 15 out of every 100 boys who are also victimized.

Research on adults has shown that the impact of sexual assault on males is no less severe than it is on females. Male victims tend to blame themselves, feel depressed or anxious, and question their masculinity either because of their inability to fight back or the fact that they said "no" to a willing female.[74]

If boys do report a sexual assault, which is unlikely, they will run into a brick wall of indifference known as the male rape myth. Psychologists Nicola Fisher and Afroditi Pina described this myth in the context of an article about adult male victims. According to the myth, males: cannot be overpowered or forced to have sex by a woman because they are bigger and stronger; are to blame for not fighting harder; can cope well after an assault;[75] and enjoy sex regardless of whether it is forced. Psychologist Michelle Davies describes how the heterosexual script contributes to this myth of male enjoyment:

> As socialization encourages men to seek and respond to any opportunity to engage in sexual activity with women, sexual coercion may be conceptualized as sexual experience...rather than

a violation of will.[76]

As with sexual harassment, the number of girls reporting rape was much higher than the number of boys, but boys may tend to under-report. Their reluctance to talk about it is, again based in gender stereotypes and rape myths, namely that boys or men will appear weak and unmanly if they admit to being raped or sexually assaulted in any way.

Nicola Fisher believes part of the problem facing male victims, in addition to cultural forces and stereotypes, is the conceptualization of rape itself. There is a tendency to believe that if injuries were not sustained rape could not have occurred. This myth affects victims of both sexes, but males more because cases involving male victims and female perpetrators tend to leave fewer physical scars. Rather than using physical assault, female perpetrators are more likely to use verbal intimidation or exploit a man who is intoxicated. As Fisher and others have said, the tendency to look at physical harm more than lack of consent can obscure real crimes of rape and sexual assault.[77]

The fundamental cultural conception, then, is that men and boys do not suffer assault or harassment. This notion is reinforced by the fact that the topic of male sexual assault and harassment rarely makes headlines. When sexual assault and rape statistics are reported in the news, the focus is most often on the number of female victims. There is generally little acknowledgement that men and boys are assaulted and harassed too, and sometimes by females.

On the rare occasions that pop culture broaches the topic of males as victims, the harassment or assault is not presented as problematic. In fact, in the few instances I have seen recently, it has been brushed off as no big deal.

The television program *Supernatural* has included multiple scenes of men kissed and groped against their will or manipulated into sex. As with its female victims, this series ignores the larger issue of consent but when men are involved, it sometimes goes further, showing characters laughing about the incidents, as Dean does in the season one episode "Shadow." He and his brother are tied to a chair by a woman who proceeds to writhe against Sam while kissing him against his will, yet brother Dean simply jokes that the next time Sam wants to "get laid" he should find a woman who is not so crazy.[78]

And then there is the Castiel incident outlined in chapter 4. In the climactic scene, the reaper—occupying the body of April to whom Castiel lost his virginity the night before—ties Castiel to a chair with his arms behind his back. Castiel is clearly angry that he was used in the manner he was, but the reaper taunts him by straddling him and saying she found him attractive. She then cuts open his shirt with a knife and later uses the same knife to slash him multiple times before delivering a final, fatal blow. Not exactly a happy story, but in the end, after Castiel is brought back from the dead, lead character Dean laughs that the one-time angel "gave it [his virginity] up to a reaper."[79] And the body that reaper occupied? Dead as a doornail, not that anyone gave her a second thought until a few episodes later when, yet again, the whole situation was given the "bro code" treatment. Dean and Sam Winchester were having a beer with Castiel who mentioned something April had told him. The dialogue proceeded as follows:

> **Castiel:** Well, Bartholomew wants to reverse Metatron's spell, presumably retake Heaven once his following is large enough. That's according to April.
> **Dean:** The reaper you banged.
> **Castiel:** Yeah, and you stabbed.
> **Dean:** Yeah. She was hot.
> **Castiel:** So hot. And very nice. Up to the point she started torturing me.
> **Dean:** Yeah. Well, not every hookup's perfect. (Dean then pats Castiel on the arm and grins.)[80]

No regret. No remorse. Clearly Castiel is over whatever bothered him about his encounter with April, as he revels in the fact that he "banged" a hot woman.

For its part, *Family Guy* is an equal opportunity offender, depicting male sexual violation as just as funny as female violation. Lead male character Peter has been raped by a "breeding bull"[81] and was shown being assaulted by the steam from a pie—ridiculous, yes, but the scene made light of him being thrown to the ground and having his pants ripped off before making a further joke about his male neighbour being forced to watch.[82]

Scenes like these are symptomatic of the way male sexuality is treated in our media and wider culture. Self-sufficient, sexually precocious, and physically tough, boys are thought to be immune to any kind of sexual violation.

This toughness is also thought to be a bulwark against worries over body image, another misconception about boys born of male stereotypes.

Chapter 6—Size Does Matter

> "...American men are nearly as dissatisfied about their bodies as women and experience depression and self-esteem problems that are partly due to gendered cultural standards, some of which are produced by media."
>
> *Kari Lerum and Shari L. Dworkin*[1]

For boys growing up in Western society, there is no escaping the message that size matters. From sports broadcasters chirping about the height and weight of professional athletes—especially in North American football—to David Beckham and various Calvin Klein models showcasing their physical endowments in risqué underwear ads, boys and men are, as Lerum and Dworkin note above, feeling the pressure of culturally generated body image ideals.

It is not just about muscles either. In a culture dominated by the heterosexual script, the responsibility for "good" sex is assigned to males. Feeling the need to be experts yet lacking adequate sexual education, many young men turn to X-rated films for guidance and are greeted with scenes of impossibly huge male sex organs that never fall limp, despite hours of action. It is quite a standard to live up to. Indeed, as social psychologist Petra Boynton has found in working with her male clients, many men feel threatened and inadequate in a culture that "defines modern masculinity by successful sexual performance, stamina, and stiffies."[2] Few studies have been done on adolescent male sexual anxiety, but, as we will see, the fears men express in their adult years often have their roots in teenage experiences with erotic imagery and films.

The Sexualization of Male Bodies

The push for male physical perfection is not new. Among the first to promote male muscularity as an ideal was Charles Atlas with his famous exhortation against "97-pound weaklings." The era in which Atlas first began marketing his fitness products was one of pin-up girls;[3] male bodies were rarely, if ever, eroticized in calendars and posters. The Charles Atlas ads may have shown the muscled guy getting the girl, but there was nothing overtly sexual about the presentation of the man. The emergence of the *sexualized* male body in advertising began in the 1980s, led by Calvin Klein and his notorious underwear ads featuring muscular men in nothing but their briefs. Feminist philosopher Susan Bordo recalls that the placement of the first of these Calvin Klein ads in Times Square in New York led to huge sales and widespread theft of smaller posters of the ad from bus shelters.

At this point, consumer culture discovered the "commercial potency" of sexual representations of the male body. Hollywood and other fashion houses would follow suit in the years to come,[4] a trend noted by cultural theorist and media commentator Rosalind Gill who said in a 2005 article that "men's bodies *as bodies* have gone from near invisibility to hypervisibility," on display in action films, fashion and cosmetics ads, and the covers of magazines like *Men's Health*. She wrote as well that "...it is not simply that the *number* of images of the male body has increased; more significant is the emergence of a *new kind of representational practice* in mainstream popular culture, depicting male bodies in idealized and eroticized fashions."[5] (Italics in the original text.)

Indeed. The "perfect" male physique is taking up more space in our media environment. Even if not directly eroticized, these ideal male bodies are associated with sexual success. As psychologist Marika Tiggeman notes, media do not present body ideals in isolation. Perfect bodies are part of complex cultural scripts that link muscularity (or thinness in women) to happiness, desirability, and status.[6] This link between appearance and sexual attractiveness exerts a powerful influence on impressionable adolescents.

As with women, advertising is one of the main sources of sexualized male bodies. Retailer Abercrombie & Fitch (A&F) was one of the most well-known exploiters of male bodies, having produced several ads that not only sexualized but also objectified men. Case in point: a February 2013 visit to the Abercrombie & Fitch website showed a bare-chested, muscular young man with unbuttoned pants slung an almost indecent distance below his waist. His face was not shown and his body was positioned at a slight angle to the viewer—not full-out canting as per Erving Goffman's definition, but not quite squared to the camera either. This man, like many others in the company's history, was clearly being sexually objectified. (In November, 2015 the company launched its first campaign under its new branding strategy, which was designed specifically to minimize sexualized imagery.[7])

A&F sells clothing so their erstwhile emphasis on the body—however objectifying—was to some degree understandable. But it is not just fashion retailers getting in on this game. Sellers of more mundane products have begun to use male bodies as a marketing tool, following the lead of companies that have, for decades, used female bodies in this manner.

In 2013 the male body was used in campaigns to promote air fresheners, salad dressing, and tequila.[8] More recently, the makers of Stone Tile have used muscular men sporting the garb of contractors—jeans, tool belt, and work boots—to market their brand of floor tiles.[9]

The salad dressing ads, in particular, received a considerable amount of attention, largely because of the suggestive poses of the male model. Known as the "Zesty Guy," the model was shown shirtless in some television and print ads but bared more in others. In one ad, he was shown lying on the ground completely naked, save for a strategically placed picnic blanket.[10] In another he was pictured wearing nothing but an apron, lying seductively on a table with his finger in his mouth.[11] *Adweek* magazine referred to this trend as "hunkvertising" and cited copywriter Rebecca Cullers who wrote: "What should worry men about these portrayals is that there's really only one kind of guy being held up as 'hot'…It's dangerous to limit the notion of attractiveness to a single model."[12] Women no doubt shouted a collective and sarcastic, "You think?" upon reading that passage.

Men are showing more skin on television as well, including Oliver Queen of *Arrow*, who seems to spend at least half of each episode naked from the waist up. The program's Instagram feed also features numerous photos of shirtless male characters. Although only 90 seconds long, the 2015 trailer for Netflix's new *Daredevil* series showed protagonist Matt Murdock's bare torso. He is not as large as some in the superhero genre but his six-pack was clearly visible.[13] Reality programs also show their share of male chests, including the various incarnations of MTV's *The Real World* series and *Slednecks*.

Movies are another source of perfectly shaped male bodies. At the time of writing, the film *Magic Mike XXL* had just begun its promotional cycle. The release of its trailer made headlines on the websites of such serious news outlets as Canada's CBC, *The Guardian*, CNN, *Time*, *The Washington Post*, and even *The Wall Street Journal*, along with the usual entertainment and gossip sites. The trailer was focused heavily on the male physique and packed plenty of pelvic thrusts into its very brief running time.[14]

Although less sexualized, the superhero genre puts hyper-muscled bodies front and centre. Superheroes need bodies that demonstrate their physical strength but even they take things to extremes. As an example, we can compare past incarnations of Superman to the most recent filler of the red and blue suit, Henry Cavill. A simple Google search will suffice, but you can go further and search for the Superman computer wallpaper I found which showed all of the actors who have played Superman in one image, in chronological order. The difference in muscle definition and chest-to-waist ratio from the 1960s to now is shocking.[15] When you add in Thor, Captain America, and Wolverine, you have some pretty heavy heavyweights.

Male celebrities are also doing more of the body-centric posing that has, in the past, been the province of females. Consider Justin Bieber. Although derided by most adults, he maintains a considerable fan base, all of whom are transfixed by his transformation from mop-topped teen of slight build into a seriously muscled young man. His new physique was showcased in a 2015 Calvin Klein Jeans advertising campaign that featured several images of his "six-pack,"[16] and a Calvin Klein underwear ad that showed more of his assets. Later stories suggested there was some editing involved in the underwear ad, particularly in the area immediately below the waist. An animated GIF claimed to show the editing of his "bulge" but it is not definitive proof. As for his muscular frame, a January 2015 picture on Bieber's Instagram feed verified that it is real, although possibly enhanced for the Calvin Klein ad.

A few months prior to the Bieber video and photos, pop star Nick Jonas of Jonas Brothers fame was featured in *Flaunt* magazine, showing off his chiselled torso and, in a series of underwear shots, holding his penis to accentuate its size.[17] The magazine might not appeal to teens but, much like the trailer of *Magic Mike XXL*, the media coverage of the photos likely caught their attention. The Jonas article was mentioned by *Billboard*, *Entertainment Tonight*, Ryan Seacrest, *The Huffington Post*, *E!* News, TMZ, and other gossip media. The same media outlets gave considerable attention to the Bieber ads as well.

And then there are the sports and fitness magazines. Although many cover shots showcase men's torsos to the top of the pubic bone, the images in these publications are not completely sexualized. They do, however, promote the idea that sexy means "ripped," with frequent headlines about sexual performance accompanying the flawless bodies on the covers. For example, the February 2014 issue of *Men's Health* promised to show men how to get "RIPPED RIGHT NOW," and also offered advice on how to solve bedroom blunders. Similarly, in June 2015 *Men's Fitness* commanded readers to "Get Ripped Now!" while also learning how to "flip her sex switch." And the January/February 2015 issue of *Men's Fitness* implored men to lose their guts, and also claimed to have the inside track on sex secrets that would "blow her mind." Between the text and the pictures, these magazine covers connect the dots between a hard body and a good sex life.

According to sociologist Rosemary Ricciardelli and colleagues, this kind of exposure is dangerous because it promotes a certain body type as an ideal and places men and boys at risk of "falling into the same appearance-orientated cultural trap that women have experienced for years."[18]

While the outcomes of this trap might be the same—body shame and dissatisfaction—the experiences of males and females are different. Girls with low body-esteem feel pressure to be thin and buxom while boys with poor body image can suffer at both ends of the scale. Overweight boys typically want to be thinner while smaller boys may strive to be more muscular. Even boys of average weight are affected: according to one 2011 study, nearly 31% of average-weight boys wanted to be bigger.[19]

The reason is obvious and unchanged since the days of Charles Atlas: muscles are associated with masculinity, something boys feel compelled to prove at all stages of their life but especially as they enter adolescence. As psychologists Linda Smolak and Jonathan A. Stein note, adolescence is a time when teens feel more pressure to conform to societal expectations about gender. Boys, in particular, may feel the need to show physical proof of their strength and athleticism since those two traits are so intertwined with conventional views of masculinity and, increasingly, male sexual appeal. [20]

Pediatrician Marla Eisenberg and colleagues conducted a study into how often boys and girls (mean age 14.4) had used muscle-enhancing behaviours in the previous year to increase their muscle size or tone. The teens were asked to indicate whether they never, rarely, sometimes, or often did things like changing their eating, exercising more, taking protein powder or shakes, or using steroids or other muscle-enhancing substances like creatine, amino acids, or growth hormones.

The study showed that the majority of boys chose exercise as a means to increase muscle: 81% sometimes or often used exercise compared to 63.8% of girls. Drilling down a bit further, we see that 40.9% of boys "often" used exercise to improve muscle tone compared to 27.3% of girls. The discrepancies between males and females are even sharper when it comes to the more extreme behaviours. Between the "sometime" and "often" users:

- nearly 19% of boys reported using protein powders (12.4% sometimes and 6.3% often), compared to 8.2% of girls (6.2% sometimes, 2% often)
- just over 3% of boys used steroids (2.3% sometimes and .8% often), compared to just over 1% of girls (0.9% sometimes and 0.3% often)
- 6.4% of boys used other muscle-building substances (4% sometimes and 2.4% often), compared to just over 2% of girls (1.6% sometimes and 0.7% often).[21]

Although the percentages for the most extreme behaviours were relatively low for both sexes, the boys' numbers are significant. Important as well is the 17% difference between boys and girls using exercise to increase muscle. Clearly the building of muscle, while of concern to some girls, is a much bigger issue for boys. And if Major League Baseball player Bryce Harper is any sort of example, the pressure on boys may be getting worse. The Washington Nationals right fielder appeared on the cover of the 2015 edition of *ESPN Magazine*'s Body Issue. As per the mandate of the issue, his body was the focus and it looked as chiselled as one would expect. The problem is the extreme actions he took to make his body look the way it did. He is clearly a man in excellent physical condition, but that wasn't enough for him. The *Huffington Post* outlined the regimen he followed in the days leading up to the photo shoot:

> [Harper's preparation] consisted of three workouts and six meals a day until it consisted of none, that final week when Bryce Harper consumed only juice. Seven different raw juices. Over the final two weeks, before he exposed each of his muscles to ESPN's photographers, he put salt in his drinking water so he could hydrate himself without gaining weight.
>
> On the final day, before he stripped naked and recorded the results for the world, he rose for one final workout, but when he went to refresh himself, he spit the water out. When he arrived at the field at the University of Nevada Las Vegas for the shoot, his system was completely depleted. He shoved raw, white potatoes down his throat because he knew the glucose and glycine they contained would run straight to his muscles — which yearned for something, any kind of nourishment they could find.
>
> "It makes you pop," Harper said. "It makes you stand out."[22]

In the article journalist Lucy McCalmont described Harper's actions as "grueling and seemingly dangerous." That is an understatement. Comparing Harper to Kevin Love, an NBA player who also appeared in the issue, McCalmont noted that Love did nothing out of the ordinary ahead of his photo session. There is a four-year age gap between Love and Harper—not huge but perhaps enough to show evidence of a generational shift in attitudes about body image.

Examples from pop culture and the world of sports show how male bodies are currently depicted, but it is important to realize that media affects boys in different ways. Other factors contribute to boys' body esteem, including the degree the internalization of body ideals, peer influence, and a boy's pubertal development or lack thereof.

Internalization is the degree to which people adopt cultural body ideals into their own beliefs about what is physically attractive. Levels of internalization are tested with a standard questionnaire (SATAQ-3) that asks participants to indicate their level of agreement with statements like: "I would like my body to look like the people who are in the movies" or "I compare my body to that of people who are athletic."[23] Unsurprisingly, recent studies with adolescent boys have found that those who internalize body ideals have lower body-esteem.[24,25]

These body ideals are omnipresent in our media, as I showed above, but Tiggeman's research on television's impact shows that not everyone who sees idealized bodies internalizes them. Her 2005 study discusses two factors that contribute to internalization: what kids are watching and why. Programs that contain more "realistic" portrayals—like soap operas in her day and, I would surmise, some of the soapier superhero and reality programs today—affect boys' drive for muscularity because they send the message that romantic success comes from physical appearance. The reasons for watching are also a factor: teens who use television for social learning, particularly about behavioural and appearance standards, are more likely to internalize the body ideals they see and experience negative body image.[26]

Media portrayals are not the only route for body ideal internalization. Peers also play an important role, often by reinforcing the messages media sends. A few recent studies have drawn similar conclusions about peer influence:

- Psychologists Diana Carlson Jones and Joy K. Crawford[27] looked at the "peer appearance culture" that surrounds adolescents. They found that boys face a high degree of appearance pressure and teasing from their peers, and even perceive more of such pressure than girls. For boys, appearance pressure includes suggestions for body change and critical comments about muscularity, as in, "You're too skinny." Teasing can affect boys directly and indirectly: even if they are not a target, they may feel pressure from witnessing the teasing that other "97-pound weaklings" endure.
- Looking at boys aged 8-11, psychologist Lina Ricciardelli and colleagues concluded that even the perception of pressure to

increase muscles from parents, close friends, or media increased the likelihood boys would be concerned about their weight and take steps to improve their muscularity.[28]
- Psychologist Trent Petrie and colleagues found that sociocultural pressures to be muscular were especially salient to boys.[29]
- In a 2011 study, psychologists Margaret Lawler and Elizabeth Nixon—echoing Carlson Jones and Crawford—noted that peer appearance criticism had an impact on boys' body image and concluded that the peer group is "an an important vehicle for the transmission of socio-cultural messages of appearance ideals."[30]

For boys, appearance-based teasing centres on excessive weight, absence of muscle tone, or small stature in general. With or without teasing, boys are keenly aware of whether they fit the masculine body ideal. Studies show that boys with a high body mass index or BMI (tending toward overweight) and a low BMI (tending toward smaller frames and thinness) are less satisfied with their bodies than average-weight boys.[31]

Most of us are aware of the tremendous pressures placed on overweight individuals in our society. According to Lina Ricciardelli and colleagues, children as young as seven already associate excessive body weight with being less attractive and having fewer friends. Jones and Crawford found that boys with higher BMIs tended to discuss muscle-building strategies frequently with friends, a sign of their body dissatisfaction. Boys with lower BMIs are also teased about their appearance but there is little they can do in the face of pressure to be bigger other than accept the fact that some boys are just naturally smaller than others—a tall order during adolescence when the size discrepancy between boys can be vast, largely because of the varying ages of pubertal development.

Indeed, research has shown that the timing of puberty plays a significant role in the weight-based body-esteem of boys. Boys who perceive themselves as late in reaching puberty tend to be more dissatisfied with their weight. Even those who have a similar BMI to more physically mature boys may feel unhappy with their weight, likely because being less developed means being less muscular. Late-developing boys also tend to be shorter than their peers and feel the differences in their overall size more acutely.[32]

The news does not get better as boys get older. Jones and Crawford found that appearance pressure is greater for boys in high school than middle school, especially for late bloomers.[33] It continues into adulthood as well. A study by pediatrician Alison Field and colleagues interviewed young men about body image in 1999, when they were aged 12 to 18, and followed up with them in 2011. In 1999, approximately 8.5% were "extremely concerned" about their muscularity. By the time these boys reached adulthood, 17.9% had become extremely concerned about both their weight and physique.[34] In her research, Rosalind Gill concluded that appearance-based teasing and critiques are an inevitable part of the male experience, even after adolescence. She describes the ways boys and men police the bodies of their peers, noting that contrasts with other males are "powerful and persuasive means of upholding norms of masculinity."[35]

Judgment of those norms of masculinity is based not only on the size of a man's pecs, but also his penis and its ability to perform.

Performance, Stamina, and Size

"The penis is a player on the sexual world stage—an organ of performance, a barometer of self-worth, an indicator of sexual profit and loss, and a contributor to the sexual performance index particular to each and every male, regardless of sexual orientation." So wrote sociologist Michael Kimmel and colleagues in their introduction to the *Cultural Encyclopedia of the Penis*.[36] Many men would see truth in this statement, having been taught from their teenage years onward to believe that penis size and erectile function are the ultimate signifiers of manhood. As Petra Boynton notes, men's sexual identities are "structured around performance, stamina and size" in contrast to women, for whom sex is "constructed as being a mix of the physical and emotional."[37]

The emphasis on penis size is not a modern invention. Scenes in *Fanny Hill* describe a man's "oversized" and "unwieldy machine" and the 1873 erotic novel *The Romance of Lust* describes the considerable size of the male protagonist's member.[38] Given that both novels were written by men, one can assume that a certain fixation on penis size must have existed then as it does now. This particular anxiety was captured more recently in a dryly humorous manner by psychologist Bernard Zilbergeld:

> Real men with real penises compare themselves to the models and find themselves woefully lacking. Most men believe that their penises are not what they ought to be. They are not long enough or wide enough or hard enough, they do not spring forth with the requisite surging and throbbing, and they do not last long enough or recover fast enough. A recent magazine survey of over a thousand men found that 'all male respondents, with the exception of the most extraordinarily endowed, expressed doubts about their own sexuality based on their penile size' ... The problem is that we think we should measure up to what are basically impossible standards ... Accepting your own merely human penis can be difficult. You know it is somewhat unpredictable, and, even when functioning at its best, looks and feels more like a human penis than a battering ram, or mountain of stone. Not much when compared to the fantasies you are brought up on.[39]

Those fantasies are based on the "pornographic penis," which, according to cultural studies professor Stephen Maddison, has never been "bigger or harder" than it is in current XXX films. In porn, the process of attaining male arousal is completely absent, so as to avoid showing anything other than the "mountain of stone" Zilbergeld described—no limp penises allowed. Male porn actors are always fully erect and ridiculously well-endowed, a "biological fiction" in Maddison's words,[40] achieved through various tricks of the film trade. Porn men are also shown as "always sexually willing and able to perform sexually for hours,"[41] another imperative in our culture where the erect penis is "manhood personified" and the flaccid penis is "femininity in a male organ, all abject vulnerability and failure."[42]

Even if boys and men recognize the considerable distortions in porn—and most do—their anxieties remain, in part because they have no understanding of what constitutes a normal penis or sex drive.

As we saw in chapter 3, sexual education is of dubious value to boys, and doctors rarely inquire about their male patients' sexual health or offer any kind of guidance about sexual activity when boys reach their teenage years. To answer questions about how their penises should look and behave, many boys turn to media depictions, whether in pornography or elsewhere.

As a result of the exaggerated images they see, many boys and men overestimate average penis size and underestimate their own size,[43] leading many who are perfectly normal to believe they are far from adequate.

A 2005 study by Rany Shamloul, a specialist in andrology and sexual medicine, showed that an overwhelming majority of participants thought they had a short penis, but none actually did.[44] Even men who consider themselves "average" are not necessarily happy with their size. In research by sociologist Janet Lever and colleagues, 46% of men who believed they had an average-sized penis wanted it to be bigger. Further, only 54% of these "average" men were satisfied with their size, compared to 86% of men who considered themselves "large." Men who saw themselves as small had it even worse—only 8% were satisfied with their penis size. Lever's study also showed that men who think they have a below-average penis may become self-conscious and less likely to undress in front of their partners or let their partners see their penis during sex.[45]

Recent research has shown that the impact of "small penis syndrome" may extend beyond the bedroom. Studies are ongoing but a survey of male and female post-secondary students showed that men with a healthier perception of their penises had lower levels of sexual anxiety and self-consciousness, and higher sexual esteem.[46] The report by Lever and colleagues also found a possible link between perceived penis size and body satisfaction: men who think they have large penises rate their faces as more attractive and feel much happier with their bodies overall than men who believe their penises are small.[47]

What role does media play in small penis syndrome? We've already seen pornography's distortions of penis size and performance, but other media reinforce that message. A few recent examples stand out.

The very popular 2014 film *Ride Along* includes plenty of the female objectification typical of the "buddy cop" genre—montages that emphasize the cleavage and legs of the female lead, a scene in a strip club—but there is also commentary on men's physical assets. Dedicated to his fiancée, lead male Ben is far from the stereotypical, promiscuous male but feels the need to do a little bragging, telling her that his video game nickname "Black Hammer" is a reference to the sound his supposedly huge penis makes after he drops his pants and it hits the floor: "Kaboom! Boom!" Another character, acting crazed in a farmer's market, strips down to his underwear, prompting a woman to say: "He is packing."

In music, Nicki Minaj refers to a "dude" having a "dick bigger than a tower" in her hit *Ananconda*, a song that samples Sir Mix-A-Lot's infamous *Baby Got Back* and the lyric that compares his penis to an anaconda. Staying on the snake theme, Flo Rida references his "cobra" in *GDFR*, a top ten song on the Billboard Hip-Hop chart in early 2015.[48] In *No Mediocre*, T.I. talks about his "pipe" being so big that women have trouble sitting down the morning after being with him.[49] Clearly very proud of his size, T.I. raps in mega-hit *Blurred Lines* that he would give a woman "something big enough to tear [her] ass in two." The video for the song also includes the message that Robin Thicke has a "big dick."[50] A tongue in cheek reference? Perhaps, but it still makes it clear that size matters.

Beyond popular culture, Boynton believes some of the blame for male sexual anxiety lies with the pharmaceutical industry which has created exacting standards of performance for the penis: "It must get hard when desired, stay hard as long as required, and be able to regularly repeat this exercise."[51]

Lad magazines include plenty of ads for products that promise to improve performance and increase penis size,[52] as do other men's magazines. In addition to erectile dysfunction drugs like Viagra, Levitra, and Cialis, there are also "herbal" remedies. I saw one such ad on the "Sex & Women" page of the *Men's Health* website in February of 2015. The advertisement read "KEEP IT UP. Conquer low T and revitalize your life." The ad clicks through to keepitupbook.com, a site that tells visitors they can "once again have it all—the muscle, the emotional drive, the sexual power, the vigor and cognitive sharpness that you enjoyed when you were a younger man." The program claims to involve "crucial supplements," "hormone optimization," and "stuff you may never learn from your family doctor."[53] Ad copy like that is a big red flag in my eyes, but would likely appeal to men who have fallen prey to media messages about the importance of optimizing their bedroom performance.

It is not just advertising contributing to male sexual anxiety but the general content of men's magazines as well. We have seen how these publications objectify women and fixate on their appearance, but they also target men's insecurities. Magazines like *Men's Health* and *Men's Fitness* focus on exercise and fitness but also devote considerable space to the discussion of penises and sexual performance.

In February, 2015 I searched "penis size" on the website of *Men's Health* magazine. It was hard to gauge the volume of articles since there were many duplicates in the 507 search results, but what caught my attention were the themes that emerged. Articles included: "Your Perfect Penis Size;" "What's an Average Penis;" "Is My Penis Normal;" and "Penis Size and Sexual Satisfaction." On the home page of the site I also saw several headlines pertaining to performance: "8 Ways to Protect Your Erection;" "Make Missionary Sex Incredible;" "Make Doggy Style Even Hotter," and, my personal favourite, "How to Have Sex for an Hour!" The latter theme was picked up on by *Men's Fitness* in an article entitled "Too Quick(ie)" which offered expert advice on how long women want to have sex. (The recommended time is considerably less than the hour suggested in the *Men's Health* headline: 20 minutes is considered ideal while anything less than 7 minutes is thought to be rather lacking.)

Adding to the ego-bruising for men are the numerous articles purporting to share women's opinions on men's penises. These examples come, again, from *Men's Health*: "Penis Size: What Women Think," "Women's Penis Size Preference," "Her Thoughts on Your Penis," and "What She Thinks About Your Body."

Some of these articles deal with genuine health concerns but are couched in language that heightens readers' insecurities while also reinforcing the notion that the responsibility for "good" sex lies with men. The overall message? If a man doesn't measure up or happens to "misfire" [54] before his partner climaxes, he has somehow failed.

Messages about male size and performance may be resonating with young people. Pediatricians Michael Westwood and Jorge Pinzon noted that adolescent boys may have an "unfounded perception" of normal or desirable penis size, especially if they have watched pornography or seen advertisements for penis enlargement products.[55] Other research bears out the conclusions of Westwood and Pinzon: two recent studies show that about 40% of adult men trace their problems with penis size to adolescence and their experiences watching erotic films.[56, 57] Sociologist Marshall Smith came to a similar conclusion. He conducted detailed interviews with young adults about their experiences with sexually explicit online material during their adolescence. Many respondents—both male and female—reported learning from these media that males are responsible for women's sexual pleasure, an expectation that many men said led to anxiety and stress.[58] Other men blamed their lack of sexual self-esteem on teasing about penis size or performance by a classmate or teenage romantic partner.[59]

Raised on impossible standards of size and performance, boys, like girls before them, are increasingly questioning their physical attractiveness and taking steps to remedy their perceived bodily imperfections. As male bodies are increasingly eroticized and objectified in our culture, this problem stands to get worse.

Now, more than ever, our sons need to be shown the value of critical thinking and the importance of questioning the peer and media influences around them. Who better to guide them than their own parents?

Chapter 7—What Parents Can Do To Combat Sexualized Media Messages

> Sexual socialization is the "intricate and gradual process by which young people acquire knowledge, attitudes, and values about sexuality through the integration of information from multiple sources."[1]
>
> *Deborah Fisher*

How do kids learn about sex? Certainly there is a biological drive behind their interest, but the finer points about when to initiate sexual activity and how to have a sexual relationship are acquired through a process of social learning, similar to the one that teaches morals, ethics, social practices, and even basic skills. To put it simply, children watch others and learn from them.

In the case of sexual socialization, multiple influences are at play, as Deborah Fisher notes in the passage above. Young people take in cues from the popular culture and media that surround them, and the attitudes and behaviours of their peers and parents.

As we've seen throughout this book, the masculine imperative and heterosexual script that dominate our media and wider culture can have considerable negative influence on boys' sexual socialization. Boys are given fewer opportunities than girls to educate themselves about their sexuality, yet are encouraged seek any and all opportunities to have sex. They are not taught to value their emotions or those of their partner but told, instead, that sex is a casual, physical game with girls as the pawns; a "collection of body parts existing for male pleasure," in the words of educational psychologist Lori Day.

It is difficult for boys to counter the pressure to conform to social norms about sex. Peers reinforce what popular culture communicates and boys who challenge or disregard prevailing notions about the male sexual role risk being ostracized, called names, or even sexually harassed themselves for not being suitably masculine.

What can we, as parents, do to help our sons combat the negative messages in their social environment and media? Understand our power and learn how to use it. I've included some tips and strategies here, organized by the themes and topics discussed in prior chapters.

Parents Have Power

Among all of the influences on boys' understanding of sex and sexual roles, media is the primary point of concern for most parents. Their worries are justifiable, given the media environment I described in the previous chapters. Yet, contrary to what many parents have been led to believe, the effects of media are not "hypodermic."[2] That is, kids do not blindly follow the lead of celebrities and fictional characters when it comes to sex.

Media cannot be discounted entirely, however. They help establish norms, fill in gaps in knowledge, and model behaviour that some young people may be keen to emulate.

Even if kids don't act out what they see, their attitudes may change and they may become part of the problem by, for example, ignoring sexting and harassment, or being bystanders in general to others' bad behaviour.

The burning question for most parents is this: can the lessons provided by Mom and Dad outweigh media messages? The short answer is a resounding yes.

Over the years, a variety of theories have been put forth to explain media influence on children's attitudes and behaviours. Although each theory differs in the details, they all share one fundamental point: responses to and absorption of media messages depend on many factors unique to each child's experience. Media are certainly a major influence for some, but for others, peers and parents play an important role as filters of media messages. The reasons for using media also come into play. Children who use media to learn about a subject (like sex) pay more attention and may place more value on what they see and hear, while those seeking entertainment may take media messages less seriously.

The bottom line in all of the research I read, however, is that parents have power. In fact, Deborah Fisher believes that parents are the "foremost" influence in a child's sexual socialization. Other researchers concur. Here is what some recent studies have said about the parental role in sexual socialization:

- Children whose parents have expressed disapproval of teen sex show lower levels of sexual initiation and lower frequency of vaginal intercourse.
- If parents monitor their kids by talking regularly with them, knowing who their friends are and what do when they hang out, their children will be less likely to start having sex at an early age.
- The absence of parental attention is also a form of influence: poor relationships with parents can lead children to initiate sexual activity at a younger age, perhaps to compensate for the lack of emotional and physical connection in their families.
- Parents who watch and critique media with their children can affect their kids' attitudes toward sex in a positive way. [3,4,5]

In short, there are many opportunities for parents to guide their sons and help them make smart decisions about sex. In the remainder of this chapter I will talk about specifics, but first, a few words about communication and media literacy.

Communication

Communication is fundamental to all human relationships, yet it is something many people struggle with. Parents and teenagers have particular challenges in this area, especially when those teenagers are boys.

I hear from a lot of parents that their boys never want to talk. Many parents throw up their hands in the face of this reticence, conditioned to believe that boys are wired differently and inherently less capable of talking than girls. In reality, many boys love to talk but grow up in a culture that discourages them from doing so.

As we have seen, the masculine imperative dictates that boys should be stoic and self-reliant, two factors that mitigate against effective communication. Boys are not often invited to talk, whether about school, friends, or life in general. If they aren't in the habit of talking about this "easy" stuff, it is much harder to open a dialogue about sex.

So how do you get boys talking?

It is easiest if you start young so you can get boys accustomed to talking, but even if you are starting later, you can still help your son get comfortable with the idea of communicating. Here are some ideas, tips, and experiences of my own for reference:

- Conversations don't have be complicated or deep. Engage boys in chats about everyday life—what happened at school today, what are you learning in various subjects, what did you do at recess? We have these sorts of conversations daily at the dinner table or on the walk home from school and our sons participate fully. Our chats are casual and light but also make clear to our sons that we want to hear what they have to say. Talk about your day too so this becomes a two-way conversation that encourages questions and feedback from your son.
- Ask follow-up questions and really engage with your son to create further conversation. Once the floodgates open, these seemingly idle conversations can go off in many directions and lead to more sensitive subjects or areas of concern he might have.
- Don't turn conversations into inquisitions. There's no need to grill boys over every detail of the daily happenings at school or what they did when they were hanging out with friends. Kids will get defensive, and rightly so. During your chats with your son you are building trust and setting the expectation that he can talk to you and you will listen without judgment. Keep your chats informal and non-confrontational.
- Listen when he talks and give serious attention to what he says, especially if he seems concerned or worried about something.

- Be patient if he seems troubled but doesn't want to talk about what is bothering him. Boys are sensitive to social norms about being a "man" and may feel the need to appear in emotional control. Unless you think there is an urgent need to resolve an issue, give your son time and space to process what he is feeling and invite him to talk whenever he is ready.

TIP: Don't force conversation, especially on an older boy who may not be used to a lot of talk. Meet him where he lives, as the saying goes, perhaps by starting with things he is passionate about: sports, books, games, school, or whatever gets his attention. In our house, baseball never fails to be a conversation starter and a comment as simple as "How about those Blue Jays" is often the launching point for a very long and interesting chat.

Conversations with your son are invaluable. They strengthen your relationship, normalize the act of communication, and make it far easier to transition from mundane topics to trickier subjects like sex.

Media Literacy

Conversations about media can be touchy. It is during adolescence that kids start to forge their own identity. They often use pop culture to signal who they are, carefully selecting musical artists, television shows, films, video games, and even books that make a certain statement. Often, the more parents dislike something, the more appealing it becomes to a teen. Music is a common flashpoint for parents and children, with many kids choosing artists that push the envelope with language and overtly sexual themes, but other areas of popular culture can also inflame parents.

The word "no" is often the knee-jerk response of parents faced with content they deem inappropriate or too mature, sexist, or sexual. Many parents also fall into the "because I said so" trap without offering further detail about why they disagree with a particular choice. For young children, the word "no" is a perfectly acceptable strategy. For older kids who have a better sense of the world and more wherewithal to question media and parental responses to it, "no" won't cut it. As Lyn Mikel Brown and colleagues wrote in *Packaging Boyhood*:

> "[N]o" shuts down discussion, and how are kids to learn if they don't have an opportunity to discuss what they like? Also, consider this: how will they be able to share what they like about their world if there's an atmosphere of impatience or criticism; how will you as a parent be able to share and listen if you can't even for a moment honor their choices but instead treat them as "bad" or "questionable"?[6]

The key phrase in that passage? Honour their choices. As parents we need to instill in our children a sense of responsibility that can come only if we let them make decisions and consider the impact of those decisions. If a boy professes his love for the song *Wiggle*, that is a personal choice. As a parent, you should not condemn that choice but talk to him about the larger implications and messages in that song and its accompanying video. The same strategy applies to all media choices, as research is increasingly showing.

Fisher and colleagues conducted a detailed study into the impact of various types of parental mediation on television viewing. They noted that while restricting access to inappropriate television programs would be the most effective option for younger children, a different approach is needed for adolescents who: see more sexual content; are interested in acquiring sexual information; and at a stage of cognitive development where they can better understand "the concepts of risk, consequences, and future planning." Their suggestion? Parental co-viewing and discussion, which enable parents to explain the content their children watch, talk about negative consequences, and reinforce positive or "desirable" messages.[7] (For the record, I am not including pornography in this point. That is a whole other issue, discussed separately below.)

Extrapolating Fisher's research to all media, the key message is that being aware of your children's media choices and discussing your concerns is a far more effective strategy for managing media than outright bans. Discussion is the basis of media literacy, not turning something into the ever-tempting forbidden fruit. Even if your child continues to watch or listen to media you dislike, he will do so with more critical eyes and ears.

Ideally, lessons in media literacy should start early in life, a point reinforced in an email chat I had with educational psychologist Lori Day. She noted that media often "scoop" parents, and "the key is to try to get out ahead of it, even if it feels uncomfortable [and] not to put off crucial conversations."

Begin when children are young with discussions of gender stereotypes, which form the basis of the sex role stereotypes they will see as they get older. Explain what stereotypes are: generalizations about people based on the group they belong to; in this case, male or female. The problem with stereotypes, again quoting Lori Day, is that they are limiting and leave no room for exceptions.[8] They also affect behaviour by making people feel they have to conform to the expectations of their group.

As kids get older, you can start to look more closely at music videos, lyrics, pro sports, advertising, and other media. Questions often work very effectively here: Why do pro sports need barely-dressed women on the sidelines? Why does Jason Derulo have eight women lying in bed with him in a music video? What do bikini-clad women have to do with selling hamburgers, Carl's Jr?

Even if there are no immediate answers, these questions get boys thinking about what they are seeing and how media representations can affect attitudes.

Boys interact with media every day, so your questions and discussions with your son need to be ongoing. As Melissa Atkins Wardy notes in her book *Redefining Girly*, challenging media representations is not a one-time thing; it involves many little talks and answering lots of questions.[9]

> **TIP**: Get to know your school curriculum on media literacy. In Ontario we have quite a good range of media literacy beginning in the primary grades. The grade 7 and 8 classes at our school, in particular, have had special programming on gender stereotypes, media literacy, and healthy relationships from our local sexual assault centre. Check in your area for community resources like this and inquire about their programming for schools.

Media literacy is a vital skill for children growing up in our media-saturated era. Much more has been written on this topic than I can cover here. For further reading, please see Appendix A.

Peers

Even the best parental communication and media literacy lessons may be lost in the face of peer pressure. Peers are social influencers, teaching kids which types of behaviour are appropriate or "cool." As communications scholar Kimberly Maxwell noted in a 2002 study, adolescents are particularly vulnerable to peer influence because they experience "a stressful biological event over a relatively short period of time," while also trying to form a personal identity that enables them to fit in rather than be outcasts.

Peer pressure can be immense and is often blamed for bad behaviour. As we saw in earlier chapters, boys face their own unique pressure in the form of the "bro code," a set of unwritten rules that tells them how to respond to their own sexual desires and teaches them to go along with or ignore the actions of their male peers, even if those actions are less than desirable.

When it comes to managing peer pressure, the key for us as parents is to be aware of who our children's friends are and what kinds of things they do together. This is not to suggest we spy on our kids, but rather that we check in with them and make it clear we're interested and involved in their lives.

Statistician David Y.C. Huang refers to this strategy as high monitoring. He studies the factors involved in teenage risk-taking and wrote specifically about sexual initiation in a 2011 paper. He and his colleagues described a scale of parental monitoring of teens aged 14-16. Parents who knew a good deal about their children's friends and their parents, kept tabs on who a child was spending time with, and were informed about a child's teachers and what they were studying in school were considered to have "High" levels of monitoring.

Relative to children in the High group, those in the Low group were more likely to initiate sex before the age of 14. Teens in the High group, in turn, delayed sexual initiation by an average of 1.5 years compared to members of the Low group. This delay sounds minor but is actually quite significant. As Huang notes, many important cognitive and social developments occur during each year of adolescence. Eighteen months is a long time and can result in "new levels of social awareness" that can improve a teen's "capacity to make sound judgments." Specifically, Huang and colleagues note that older teens might possess better coping and decision-making abilities as well as improved negotiation skills that could help them avoid risky sexual activities, unprotected sex, and coercive sex.[10]

> **TIP**: Peer influence is not always negative. Maxwell's research showed that, in setting social norms, peers can dissuade kids from engaging in harmful habits like smoking and potentially negative behaviours like drinking and having sex.[11] Consider your own sphere of friends. There have likely been times you have refrained from a behaviour because you know you will be judged harshly for it. Adolescents may often respond in a similar fashion, making peer pressure a positive instead of a negative.

Gender Stereotypes, Heterosexual Script, and Objectification

I mentioned social influence in the section on peers and it applies here too. Whether from media, peers, or parents, stereotyped ideas about gender and sexual roles are conveyed to children by the people around them.

Because gender stereotypes and the heterosexual script are so normalized and pervasive, they can be difficult to combat, but this is a war worth waging. Begin with some basics:

- Lessons in media literacy are an excellent place to start. Be sure to discuss the representations of each gender in everything from advertisements to professional sports, music videos, comic books, and video games. Look at physical appearance, clothing, amount of dialogue, and the traits exhibited by fictional characters or, in the case of music and sports, real people. Indicate the biases in various media. For example, you can discuss the lack of screen time for female characters; their often sexed-up or—relative to men—non-existent fashions; excessive muscles in men; objectifying words and actions by males. Ask questions, as I suggested earlier in the media literacy section. The key is to get boys to challenge media orthodoxy on gender and sexual roles. Such lessons, according to

Marshall Smith, will go a long way toward helping boys critique all of the sexualized media they see, whether pornography or less explicit genres.[12]

- On the subject of gender stereotypes, Lori Day recommends modelling egalitarian relationships at home. Teach boys from a young age that, regardless of what popular culture says, men can be just as active on the housekeeping and child care fronts as women. She also suggests that parents facilitate cross-gender play among younger children to encourage friendships and help boys and girls see each other as "more similar than different." Mixed-gender sports leagues are helpful in this regard. Boys can be encouraged to work with girls on school projects and in extra-curricular clubs and volunteer organizations. These strategies will also help boys and girls develop healthy dating relationships when they get older.
- Be careful of your gender-based judgments. Refrain from criticizing the appearance and fashion of celebrities, friends, and family—male or female. Avoid terms like "slutty" to describe a woman's manner of dress or behaviour and "stud" or other such words for males.
- Teach boys that it is normal to want to look at someone they are attracted to, but there are right and wrong ways to act on that attraction. Admiration is fine; objectification, catcalling, and unwanted physical contact are not.
- Encourage boys to educate themselves about the impact of gender and sex role stereotypes. Getting them to think for themselves about these things will be far more meaningful than having you, as a parent, tell them what to think. Give them this book as a guide or refer to the resources in Appendix A.

Pornography or SEM

We have seen in this book that pornography (also known as SEM or SEIM) is not the only, nor necessarily the biggest influence on boys' sexual socialization. Even media considered mainstream can have an enormous impact on boys' attitudes toward sex and, ultimately, their behaviour. Men objectifying women, seeing themselves as sexually insatiable, wanting sex mainly for the physical gratification, happy with casual sexual encounters; women being reduced to bodies and men increasingly treated in a similar fashion: all of these messages are being delivered to adolescent boys without them having to watch one second of porn.

Yet pornography is still influential. Teens know it is controversial, so it carries with it a very appealing element of subversion and rebellion. It is also the only medium to which sexually curious boys can turn for instruction in "real" sex. It is this educational aspect that makes pornography especially worrisome. As we saw earlier, teens who use media to learn about sex tend to be more highly engaged and more easily persuaded that what they are seeing is legitimate or accurate.

Some people argue that pornography is not entirely bad. In his quest to find out where and how young adults had learned about sexuality during their adolescence, Marshall Smith noted that pornography was helpful because it enabled young people to explore sexual behaviors safely and comfortably. He also found that teens use porn in a positive manner for masturbation and sex with their partners. Lastly, he noted that many of the young adults he surveyed were able to see porn for what it really is: completely false and even problematic in its representations of bodies and sexuality in general. Smith concluded that this critical approach helped avoid negative impacts.[13] In other words, kids who had the wherewithal to critique porn—that is, a high level of media literacy—were able to watch it and come away from it unscathed.

I share Smith's results not because I think we should let our sons heed the siren call of XXX films and watch freely, but to reiterate the importance of media literacy. It is unrealistic to think that boys will never watch pornographic films or read explicit magazines, so telling them to take what they see with a huge grain of salt will help avoid the worst impacts. And with boys being exposed to pornography at ever younger ages, the timing of these conversations is important. Waiting until they are in high school might be too late.

The first step in handling the issue of pornography is to be honest about both its appeal and your need to discuss it with your child. Don't pretend it doesn't exist or that your sweet young son won't be persuaded to watch with friends or seek it out himself. The statistics I presented earlier show that most boys are not regular users of pornography but many are exposed to it at some point and may become casual viewers. As hard as it is to admit, most of our sons will be among their number.

Conversations about pornography are very difficult. I know from my own experience, although my talk was made more awkward because my son had no idea what porn was. The term was introduced to him and his grade 6 classmates through an unnecessarily alarmist booklet about sexual abuse prevention distributed without first being previewed by school administrators. This book's glossary defined pornography as "sexually obscene writings, drawings, photographs or videos" but the word first appeared early in the book via a True/False quiz that said: "Pornography is about healthy relationships."[14] There had been no discussion of the topics in this book in his class so the content caught all of the kids off guard and forced parents to address the more inflammatory passages immediately.

Trying to explain pornography to an 11-year-old who had no concept of why people would want to watch sex was challenging, to say the least. It was uncomfortable for both of us but, I have to admit, it did break the ice.

If you are dealing with an older teenager who is more aware of what sex is, the conversation might be easier to initiate, but in all honesty, these discussions are always a little stressful. I say that not to dissuade you, however. As Lori Day wrote to me, not discussing porn "doesn't make it go away—it just leaves kids to navigate it alone, without parental guidance and the filter of parental values."

So where do you start?

You first have to decide the age for this conversation. You know your son and his level of maturity and sexual knowledge, so you are the best judge. Of course, your hand might be forced if your child accidentally encounters porn or, as mine did, a badly written sex ed guide.

It is essential that you be completely frank. As awkward as it is, you need to explain why people watch pornography and what concerns you have about it. It may be helpful to have those concerns mapped out before you talk. In language suited to his age, you can tell your son that most pornography:

- shows sex as an act of male aggression, with women presented as submissive and deserving of or enjoying the abusive treatment they receive;
- can be overtly violent and degrading to women, as in the case of gonzo porn and several other genres;
- distorts male sexual performance capabilities and penis size;

- is only about getting off, not actually having a relationship like a boy would in his own life;
- normalizes risky sexual acts like having sex without condoms or engaging in unorthodox sexual behaviours;
- glamourizes casual sex and promiscuity which are also risky behaviours;
- rarely if ever shows consensual encounters.

The key is to make clear the huge discrepancy between porn sex and sexual relationships in the real world. You can then talk about those "real relationships" and how they should be based on:

- understanding the potential outcomes of a sexual relationship and talking about those impacts with your partner;
- communication about what you want and when you want it;
- equal partners who share the experience together;
- freedom to say no if you'd rather not take part;
- respect for the other person's desires and wishes.

You can also talk to your son about how pornography can change his perception of what is "normal":

- Studies have found a correlation between high levels of pornography use and acceptance of aggressive sexual behaviours, like holding a girl down and forcing her to have sex, or sexual harassment.[15] Explain to your son that the sort of male sexual aggression seen in pornography is not normal. In some cases, the acts shown are criminal. Tell him succinctly and clearly that sex should not be an act of male dominance but one of equality between partners.
- Research has also shown that teens who watch a lot of pornography tend to believe that people start having sex earlier in life and prefer more unorthodox or varied sexual techniques (e.g. anal, group, bondage).[16] Tell your son it is okay to experiment sexually at the right age, but boys should draw the line at what makes them uncomfortable and not feel they have to follow the "porn script." They should also educate themselves on STI prevention for different types of sexual contact.

- Because condoms are virtually absent from pornographic films and written content, always make clear to your son that condoms must be part of his sexual experiences.
- Porn can also inhibit a boy's own sexual imagination. Rather than becoming aroused with his own thoughts and preferences, he will become more reliant on external influences and see the acts depicted in X-rated videos as more normal than his own ideas. Perhaps you can share the words of journalist Manne Forsberg who wrote in his book *Sex for Guys*:

> [S]ex is about making decisions along with your partner about trying things that are fun and exciting. It's not what you've seen online or in your tattered *Hustler* magazine. It's okay to do what you want in bed, as long as both of you help decide what to do. Porn shouldn't decide for you, and neither should anyone else, for that matter.[17]

One final, critical point that I want to reinforce here: it is vitally important that we, as parents, do not judge or condemn boys for their interest in sex. Sexual urges are natural and normal, as is the desire to see sex acted out for arousal or simply to demystify it a little. If your son is older, the message might be that you, as an adult, understand the temptation of XXX films and his interest in them, but he must be conscious of the negative messages in the films he watches. (Since porn viewing is sometimes a group activity, your son must also be told that he should never feel pressured by peers to watch anything he is uncomfortable with.)

As I noted earlier, an important part of media literacy is honouring kids' choices. It is uncomfortable to think of our sons as sexually active, but we cannot deny that they will be one day. We need to give them firm guidelines but also the freedom to learn about their own sexuality through experience. When it comes to pornography in particular, Mathias Weber's research has shown that teens who feel a lack of independence from their parents tend to use porn more. You may not want to throw open the doors to porn use, but you may wish to give an older boy some freedom so he knows that you respect his choices and believe he is responsible and capable of making sound judgments about his sexuality. If you have given him good media literacy lessons in regard to pornography and made it clear you are not watching his every move, you might even find that the allure of porn will diminish.

Of course, if you find your son showing signs of addiction to pornography, or anxiety or depression stemming from porn use, you should consult a medical professional for advice.

Sexual Health and Education

As noted above, a lot of boys will be tempted by pornography, seeking it out not only for arousal but also for instructional purposes. According to some researchers, one way to reduce the appeal of pornography is to provide adequate sexual education yourself:

- Valkenburg and Peter argue that pornography has become a "de facto" sex educator and if parents and teachers want to remain influential in adolescents' sexual socialization, they need to answer questions in "a way that keeps adolescents from consulting SEIM for sexual advice."[18] In other words, be completely open, honest, and non-judgmental about sex so you become a trusted resource for your son.
- Marshall Smith suggests giving teens general lessons on how to access sexual health information online that also cover the topic of SEM. The SEM discussions could incorporate commentary on the production of pornography, its formulaic interactions, and how different SEM is from real life,[19] thereby minimizing its perceived utility as a tool for sexual education.

In short, giving kids alternatives for their sexual education might reduce the amount of pornography they watch and keep the potential ill effects of regular porn use at bay.

Teachers can do a lot in the area of sexual education, but the approach and content can vary from school to school. As parents, it is important to know what is and is not being taught at school. We need to reiterate the lessons taught at school and fill in the gaps by engaging in discussion. We can also direct boys to accurate and informative websites and books, some of which are listed in Appendix A. Because conversations about sex between parents and sons can be uncomfortable, it may be easier to point your son to these credible and reliable resources before talking with him. Read them over first, however, to ensure they suit your values and overall approach to sexual education.

Here are some important general sexual education lessons you can convey to your son:

- Much of our culture places the responsibility for pregnancy prevention on girls. Boys need to know that they have equal responsibility and can take control of contraception themselves if a girl is unwilling or lacks adequate knowledge.
- The same message applies to STI prevention: boys can provide condoms and make sure they are used.
- Talk to boys about how STIs can be contracted and stress that oral and anal sex are not necessarily safer than intercourse.
- The predominant message in our media is that once boys get turned on, they cannot stop. Educate boys that they can and must control themselves, at least for as long as it takes to make smart decisions regarding contraception and STI prevention, and to heed the word "no" if it is uttered. Tell them to prepare themselves for those "heat of the moment" occasions when reason can fall by the wayside; that is, ensure they have condoms and use them, and instill in them a clear understanding of consent.
- Boys should not feel ashamed of the changes in their bodies, especially when spontaneous erections and wet dreams start to occur, along with the desire to masturbate. As uncomfortable as it may be, we need to reassure our sons that everything that is happening is normal and healthy, not perverted or weird.

As parents, we also need to stress the importance of sexual health care for boys. Many adults are keenly aware of the need for their daughters to see a physician on a regular basis, but less vigilant about their sons' medical check-ups. Puberty, sexuality, and body image are all areas of concern for boys. Here are some things to be aware of:

- Most schools cover the basics of pubertal physical changes, but it helps if we open the lines of communication on this topic and tell our sons they can come to us with questions. Again, a book on the subject might remove some of the awkwardness.

- Doctors tend not to be as rigorous with boys' sexual health as they are with girls'. Talk to your family doctor and let him/her know you want your son's sexual health attended to. You may, however, choose not to be present at his appointment since it may be easier for your son to talk about his concerns without you listening.
- Healthcare professionals should be attentive to boys' growth and pubertal development in their teenage years. Physicians Michael Westwood and Jorge Pinzon suggest that doctors initiate conversation by asking boys whether they have concerns over athletic performance, strength, or endurance. Such conversations can lead to questions about how a boy feels about the changes going on in his body. Parents can ask these questions too, or suggest them to their physician.
- Westwood also talks about mental health, noting that boys may be reluctant to seek care for emotional problems from fear they will appear weak. Stress, anxiety, and depression are common among adolescent boys, with pubertal changes, body image, and sexual issues sometimes at the root. Any change in a boy's disposition—increasing interpersonal conflicts, sudden poor performance in school, loss of interest in activities—should be investigated.

In addition to your family doctor, be aware of other community resources. Some organizations might run workshops and seminars about healthy relationships and boys' health care. Planned Parenthood is a good place to start. Other resources are listed in Appendix A.

Consent

How soon do we need to teach kids about consent? I have a story that might offer a few clues.

I was at a Toronto Blue Jays game in the summer of 2015 and saw a girl of about 5 years of age wrap her arms around a younger boy and give him a kiss on the cheek. The boy ended up in tears. The children's parents laughed it off and dismissed the boy's reaction as a case of him being shy. My heart went out to the little guy. He wasn't being shy; he was objecting to the unwanted physical affection. Clearly it unsettled him and may have even scared him.

Like the adults at the ball game, many people write off this type of "harmless" exchange but it is important that we do not. There is no doubt that the girl's intentions in this case were innocent but what about the little boy? It sounds extreme to say so, but his personal boundaries were violated. Imagine if the girl had been told to ask first. The boy could have said no, and an uncomfortable situation could have been avoided.

As this story shows, lessons in personal boundaries need to begin at a young age. Just as we teach kids manners and basic courtesy, we also need to teach them rules around personal space. Such lessons will carry into later childhood and adolescence. Here are a few other pointers for teaching consent at various ages:

- Model good behaviour—don't force physical affection on your own kids or anyone else. When my kids were younger I was particularly guilty of giving them an unwanted peck on the cheek or hug. I have since changed my ways and now ask before doing so. If I'm told no, I don't do it. Full stop. As psychologist Jennifer Shewmaker noted in a 2014 blog post, asking for consent before engaging in any physical affection also gives your child a chance to practice the very important actions of giving or withholding consent.[20]
- Shewmaker recommends that parents "inundate" adolescents with information on the important of consent, noting that recurring conversations are more effective than a one-time chat.
- There has been a change of focus in consent lessons lately. Instead of "no means no," the emphasis now is on affirmative consent or "yes means yes." In the documentary *Asking For It: The Ethics & Erotics of Consensual Sex*, Dr. Harry Brod puts it very clearly, in a way kids can understand: "Consent is not something you have. Consent is something the other person has to give you, and if the other person doesn't give it to you, you don't have it, no matter what you think the rules are supposed to be or what you think you're entitled to."[21] Share this lesson with kids when they are old enough to understand it.
- Because consent is rarely modelled in popular culture, it is important to talk about it when watching media with your kids. Point out the absence of consent in sexual scenes—even the least explicit ones—and explain how important it is to have clear verbal consent in any kind of physical interaction.

- Debunk the myth that boys can't stop once they've started, which is really just a masculine stereotype. Make it clear that boys can and must control their sexual urges, whether they are in an actual sexual encounter with an unwilling partner or any other situation where they feel overwhelmed by temptation.
- Explain that, despite dominant cultural messages, sex is not about a girl pleasing a boy. It is a relationship of equals, with each person's desires and wishes respected.
- Shewmaker offered another piece of good advice in her blog post: parents should include alcohol and drugs in their discussions of consent. Explaining that these substances can reduce inhibitions is important, as is the need to emphasize that consent includes the ability to make an informed decision. If someone is drunk or high, he or she will not necessarily understand what is going on and cannot consent.
- Ensure that your son knows he also has the right to say no. The heterosexual script portrays males as the initiators of sexual encounters and aggressors who always want to take things further. In reality, boys can be pushed or coerced into doing things they don't want to do and may go along because they feel they need to prove their masculinity. Boys have just as much right to stop a sexual encounter as girls and must be taught that saying "no" or "stop" is perfectly acceptable.

You can also give your son examples of how to get consent. Communication between partners is essential. These conversations are hard for teens to have, but here are a few standards they can use.

- If a boy has not yet engaged in sex with his partner, recommend that they have a discussion beforehand to see whether there is mutual interest. He needs to be clear about what he wants too. Saying "I want to take things to the next level" is not specific enough. He must specify that he is interested in sex and wanting to find out if she is too. He can keep it simple: "I really like you and I'd like to have sex sometime. Would you?" They could then progress to discussions of contraception and safe sex. It may sound unrealistic to ask this of kids, but it is best if they try to be honest and direct in their conversations about sex. Shewmaker recommends role-playing to help kids get over the unease of having these conversations.
- In the heat of the moment, a boy needs to know to pause and utter a few simple words: "Are you okay with this?" A question like this

is not too intrusive and ensures that both people are on board with what will happen next. If the answer is no, the sex stops. Period.

Remember as well that boundaries are not just physical. As I mentioned in the sections on media literacy and pornography, teens need to know their boundaries are respected when it comes to media choices and friends. Yes, you can guide them but you also have to give them space—don't check their Internet history, spy on them, or shame them for hiding a "dirty" magazine in their room. If you violate your children's privacy, your lessons on consent will seem rather hollow.

When boys and girls learn about consent at an early age, they will be less likely to confuse the issue and better equipped to challenge cultural messages of male sexual dominance and female compliance as they get older. In fact, if we start now, maybe we won't even need the "yes means yes" laws I described in chapter 4. By the time this generation gets to college or university, we can hope that the notion of seeking consent will be second nature.

Aggression/Harassment

What does it mean to cross the line? Boys are often unsure and media offers little guidance: sexually objectifying images of women are far too common; consent is rarely modelled; fictional male characters are often shown leering at women or making comments about their bodies and sexuality. Misconceptions about what constitutes "real" rape—evidenced in people's rape scripts, discussed in chapter 5—also lead to confusion over wrong and right.

A teachable moment in crossing the line came in the spring of 2015 outside a Toronto soccer game. A female reporter was setting up for a live report when the phrase "Fuck her right in the pussy" (FHRITP) was yelled at her. She confronted several young men about it, none of whom had a problem with it. When asked what his mother would think, one man said that she would "die laughing eventually." The FHRITP trend has been ongoing for a couple of years, but will hopefully die a quick death after the actions of that Toronto reporter.[22] Still, its repeated use—many female reporters interviewed after the Toronto incident said it is a daily occurrence—is indicative of the kind of culture we have created around sexual harassment and aggression, where boys and men can make crude, sexual comments and women just have to put up with them.

Boys need to understand that sexual aggression, whether verbal or physical, is never okay. They also need to learn the importance of speaking out when they see their peers engaging in any kind of harassing, aggressive, or violent behaviour. Those kinds of confrontations are difficult but essential to ending trends like FHRITP and date rapes that are common among adolescents and young adults. Here are some discussion points you can take up with your son:

- If you are watching a film or TV show, be sure to point out instances of female sexual objectification. Sexual comments directed at girls in popular culture lower the threshold for boys in the real world who might believe it is okay to treat a girl in such a manner. Make boys understand that seeing someone as a sexy plaything opens the door to aggressive or harassing behaviours.
- Ask your son to "walk a mile in her shoes" as the saying goes. Teach him to see things from the other side. How would he feel if he were a girl or woman having FHRITP yelled at him or enduring other types of harassment? Would he laugh off the comment if it were directed at his girlfriend, sister, or mother? Boys need to understand the impact of words.[23]
- Help your son combat the "bro code." Easier said than done, I know, but boys need to learn that it is not "wussy" to call out bad behaviour; it is actually very courageous. Another perspective comes from filmmaker Thomas Keith: "Think about how many lives would be improved or saved if men had the courage to say something or do something in the face of an assault, bullying, or rape."[24] Powerful words for a boy to hear.
- Teach your son to talk to others. He may not confront a peer directly but talking to another peer or trusted adult about how someone's sexual aggression bothered him can relieve some of the pressure he might feel and help him realize he is not alone in seeing this behaviour as wrong.
- Lead by example. Do not use words like "slut" and "tramp" in discussions of celebrities or friends of your son. Such labels perpetuate the "she was asking for it" mentality that underlies so many rape myths.

- A 2011 study by social workers Sarah McMahon and Lawrence Farmer showed that alcohol is often used to excuse perpetrators or blame victims of sexual assault. They suggest that rape prevention programs talk about alcohol's role in perceptions of responsibility. [25] Parents can have these conversations too, in the context of consent, and make it clear, first, that drunkenness is no excuse for committing sexual assault and, second, that someone who is assaulted when drunk is not to blame.
- Many professional sports are taking up the mantle of sexual assault prevention. Introduce them to your son. In Canada, these include the Toronto Argonauts and B.C. Lions football teams. The White Ribbon Campaign has long led this charge and has partnered with the Argonauts and others.

Boys also need to understand that they can be victims of sexual aggression and be given outlets to talk about any incidents they experience. Harassment of boys is more common than assault, although the latter does occur. Here are some ideas for handling these issues:

- Teach your son to talk to a trusted adult about any harassment directed at him. It is particularly hard for boys to take this step, given male stereotypes and the bro code, but they need to ensure the harassment stops. As we saw earlier, the impact of harassment on boys can be severe. In your conversations with your son, be sure to tell him he can come to you with any troubling behaviour and you will listen.
- Be aware that the impact of sexual harassment can be more severe than that of bullying. Schools often lump harassment under the rubric of bullying but the use of derogatory sexual language is a whole other category of abuse and should be treated as such. Boys who are called "gay" or harassed in some other sexual manner often feel deeply hurt and ashamed; having the sexual element of the crime taken out of the equation does not help and may lead people to be less understanding of how bad he is feeling. [26]
- Assure your son that the victim of harassment or assault is never to blame. Avoid saying anything that would lead him to think otherwise, for example: Were you drinking? Why did you go to that party? Why don't you stand up to the kid calling you names?
- Familiarize yourself with the sexual harassment policies in your son's school and workplace, if applicable. If he is harassed, he needs to know his rights and the courses of action open to him.

- In 2002, psychologist Michelle Davies asked a rape crisis worker about sexual assault services for males and was told: "Honey, we don't do men…Men can't be raped."[27] Given attitudes like that, it is no wonder that services for men were nearly non-existent even 15 years ago. The situation has improved but there are still far fewer options for boys and men who are victims of harassment or assault than for girls and women. If your son comes to you, help him find a qualified person to listen and support him. Many communities have a sexual assault help line, and family doctors may be able to recommend a counsellor or therapist. National hotlines might also help. I have listed some in Appendix A.

Body Image

Recently my son and I sat down to watch a short film profiling one of his favourite baseball players. At the end there was a clip of this player sitting, shirtless, at his locker. The image was on the screen for less than a minute but the man's extremely muscular frame was hard to miss.

All I could do was hope my son hadn't noticed. He aspires to be an All-Star baseball player like his idol, but the last thing I want is for him to fixate on that body type. As an elite professional athlete, this man has achieved a level of fitness unattainable to all but a few men. Yet bodies like his are the norm in sports and fitness magazines aimed at male audiences. A less chiselled but still very muscular physique can also be seen in popular musical artists like Jason Derulo, Drake, and Trey Songz, teen idols like Nick Jonas, Justin Bieber, and Shawn Mendes, and the stars of virtually any superhero film. (A look at the group from the latest *Avengers* film will demonstrate this point.) The men themselves are not to blame for normalizing this body type, but the increasing presence of that specific male physical aesthetic in popular culture makes lessons in body esteem and media literacy all the more important for boys.

As parents we need to be sensitive to the fact that boys are affected at both ends of the body shame scale: overweight boys or those who are heavy-set, but not muscular, run the risk of feeling they are too big; slimmer, smaller-framed boys may feel they are not nearly big enough.

No matter where on the size spectrum your son falls, there are some basic things you can do to help him maintain a healthy body image. The key is to remember that you have influence and, through effective communication, can help him feel secure and learn to question media depictions of male bodies. Here are some ideas:

- Do not criticize your own appearance or that of anyone else in front of your son. Conventional wisdom dictates that girls are more vulnerable to the "fat talk" or body shaming they overhear from their parents, but boys hear and internalize these messages too. The more they learn that appearance matters, the more they may pay attention to, and feel the need to compare themselves to, media images of perfect bodies.
- Point out some of the distortions boys may see in media. Marci Warhaft-Nadler notes in her book *The Body Image Survival Guide for Parents* that adult males often take on the roles of adolescents in films, creating an unrealistic basis of comparison for young audiences. For example, in *The Hunger Games* films, both Josh Hutcherson and Liam Hemsworth were playing teenagers, despite being in their 20s. In the *Divergent* film, lead actor Theo James was a full 10 years older than the 18-year-old male protagonist in the book on which the movie was based. Make it clear to boys that the "teens" they see on-screen are often adults and fully physically mature.
- Speaking of physical maturity, remind your sons often that boys develop at very different rates. When my son was in grade 7, there was a huge range of heights and muscular development among the boys; some of their voices had even changed. Ensure your son is well aware that pubertal development varies wildly between boys so he doesn't feel like he is somehow "less than." Some of the books about puberty in Appendix A might help.
- As we saw in chapter 6, peer appearance criticism can influence boys' attitudes about their bodies. Be sure to keep the lines of communication open. Talk with your son about his friends and try to gauge whether there is any ridiculing or body shaming occurring within his peer group.
- Beware of fitness and other men's lifestyle magazines. For obvious reasons, these publications focus intently on bodies. Studies have shown that these particular publications may have a negative influence on the body esteem of boys and men.[28,29,30] You may want to limit their presence in your home or discuss the content with your son.

- Boys can get sucked into hero worship habits at a very young age, either from watching sports stars or the superheroes that dominate kids' media. In most cases, heroes are associated with big, perfect bodies. Be sure to introduce your son to a wide range of male "heroes," especially those who use their brains rather than their brawn. My kids are both fans of Nikola Tesla, DaVinci, and Elon Musk (the subject of my older son's "hero" speech at school). Boys who like music might want to learn more about famous composers or musicians. And don't forget to add some accomplished females in the mix to balance a boy's definition of the word "hero."

A Strategy for Smaller Boys

Boys who are smaller than average often get teased or feel pressure to be bigger. As parents of two "small" boys, my husband and I have always been conscious of the pressures they might feel. Granted, neither is a teen yet, but we think we have laid the groundwork for high body esteem. Here are some of the things we have done:

- We find the word "skinny" just as toxic as the word "fat" and rigorously avoid its use. Words with such negative connotations should never be used to describe any child.
- We have never made size particularly relevant to our sons. We emphasize all of the wonderful things they do academically, athletically, and artistically so they don't feel their size is any more important than any other traits they possess.
- Both play sports and have had coaches and parents comment on their smaller size. (We've heard both "petite" and "diminutive" used along with the comparatively harsher "tiny.") We have told them that their size will be remarked upon but to disregard what others say. Rather than focus on their size when they play, we use words like "agile" and "quick." We have also told them that being underestimated—as small boys often are—can often work to their advantage. In short, we have framed smaller size as a positive, not a negative.

For boys in the throes of adolescence, the pressure to be muscular can intensify, a reality demonstrated by the authors of *The Adonis Complex*. They did a body image test with boys aged 11 to 17 and found that more than half preferred a body image silhouette with about 35 pounds more muscle than they actually possessed themselves: a body ideal that most men could attain only with steroids."[31] The authors recommend that parents talk with their sons about the illusions of bodily perfection in the media and the potential dangers of steroids, excessive exercise, weight-loss drugs, protein powders, and other extreme weight management and muscle building strategies. They also stress that parents not blame their sons for their desire to be bigger, but listen, understand the pressures they face, and do all they can to boost their son's self-esteem. Their book is an excellent resource for parents of boys, providing guidelines as to what constitutes extreme behaviour, and advice about how parents can help their sons accept their bodies.

> **TIP**: If your son is showing signs of extreme stress or excessive focus on his appearance, medical help might be necessary. Consult your family physician for advice.

A Strategy for Bigger Boys

With increasing numbers of kids becoming overweight, parents often have questions about how to help them achieve a healthy weight without making them feel ashamed of their appearance.

Warhaft-Nadler has some very sage advice for parents of overweight children. First, she recommends that you find out for sure if there is anything to worry about. The body ideals in our culture are so distorted that most people cannot distinguish between children who are actually overweight and those who are just on the bigger side of a healthy weight range. Schedule an appointment with a doctor without your child being present to determine if there is, in fact, a problem.

If your child is overweight, take Warhaft-Nadler's second piece of advice: say nothing. Studies have shown that focusing on a child's weight can make matters worse. Rather than addressing the issue verbally, take concrete actions that will help. Warhaft-Nadler suggests that you:

- Stay positive. Teach kids that bodies come in all shapes and sizes and the focus, always, is on healthy bodies, not skinny ones.
- Don't demonize foods as "bad." Talk about balance and moderation, and avoid making children feel ashamed for wanting a cookie or a handful of chips.
- Encourage children to get active, and get the whole family involved. In Warhaft-Nadler's words, spend less time worrying about how many calories kids are taking in and more on how many they're putting out.
- Never put children on a restrictive diet. Make healthier choices for everyone while ensuring that kids' caloric and nutritional needs are met.
- Get your son involved in menu planning, shopping, and meal preparation so he can learn to appreciate food and make good choices himself.

Sexual Anxiety

While it may not be apparent in adolescence, anxiety about penis size and sexual performance may start to take root during this phase of life. Concerns over penis size are especially common and often emerge when boys compare themselves to others, either in media or real life.

In their paper, Drs. Michael Westwood and Jorge Pinzon recommend that physicians broach the topic of penis size with adolescent male patients to ensure they develop realistic expectations in a culture that makes penis size so central to manhood. Parents can do their part as well. If your son seems concerned about his size, here is some information you can share:

- Penis size ranges greatly. Flaccid penises can range from 5 to 15 cm in length, and erect ones from 11.4 cm to 19 cm. Most men fall right in the middle of these ranges[32].
- Penile growth occurs on a very specific schedule and some boys reach their full size long before others. Locker room comparisons are unwise during adolescence or, really, any other time.
- Media, especially pornography, distort and exaggerate penis size while also sending the message that bigger is better in the bedroom. In fact, research has shown that penis size has very little to do with how much a woman enjoys intercourse. As Lynda Madaras notes in

The "What's Happening to My Body?" Book for Boys, there are no scientific studies proving that women prefer men with big penises, but there are plenty of studies that show women do not care about their partner's penis size.[33]

- If your son has seen ads for penis enlargement, explain to him that many of the techniques they promote are dangerous, then reiterate my first point about penis size: the vast majority of boys and men fall into a normal range and there is no need to worry about being bigger.

A little media literacy will help too. Stress to your son that the makers of penis enlargement products succeed only when men and boys feel badly about themselves, and they will use some rather unethical tactics to convince people that their products work.

As an example, let's consider the Male Edge™ 2nd Generation Penis Extender.[34] The home page on the company's website references a *British Journal of Urology* (BJU) report that seems to support the use of their product. The link they provide does not go to the actual study, but to the company's highly biased interpretation of the study. The BJU report actually says the efficacy of penile extenders is supported only by *"some* scientific evidence" (emphasis mine) and further studies are needed. The report also: disputes the company's claims that the extender can increase penis girth; states very clearly that these devices should only be suggested for patients who "persist" in requesting treatment even if they have a normal penis; and recommends cognitive behavioural therapy for men with anxiety about their penis size before any other treatment.[35] Not exactly a ringing endorsement. Boys should be made aware of cases like this where falsehoods are used to make products seem not only effective, but necessary.

Speak Out for Change

In this last section I am taking a page out of Melissa Atkins Wardy's book—almost literally. Wardy is a tireless advocate for girls and writes extensively about the sexualization of females in media. In her book *Redefining Girly*, she recommends that parents become advocates themselves.

Bothered by a show like *Family Guy* making fun of rape? Sick of the Sunshine Girl in the newspaper your son peruses for the sports scores? Tired of "fighting fuck toy" image of women in video games? Become an activist: blog; share your thoughts on social media; create petitions through an online tool like change.org or Care2; write letters to the editor; write to companies themselves.

Media producers love the status quo and will not change unless they know their potential audience is dissatisfied or disgusted with their product. As Wardy notes, change in the marketplace and media is not going to happen overnight, [36] but it won't happen at all if we stay silent.

Appendix A— **Further Reading**

The list below is not comprehensive, but includes resources I have come across during the research period for this book. I have divided the list by topic.

Body Image

Resources about boys and body image are few and far between, although the few I have listed here are very helpful.

Books

> Pope, Harrison et al. *The Adonis Complex: How to Identify, Treat, and Prevent Body Obsession in Men and Boys*. New York: Touchstone, 2000.
>
> *The Adonis Complex* offers a detailed look at body image issues among boys and men, with a focus on how body dissatisfaction has increased among males since the 1980s. There is a chapter dedicated to boys that talks about the extent of body image problems and the use of steroids and supplements. Although a little older than some of the resources I've listed here, this book is still an excellent resource for parents.
>
> Warhaft-Nadler, Marci. *The Body Image Survival Guide for Parents: Helping Toddlers, Tweens, and Teens Thrive*. Lemont, PA: Eifrig Publishing, 2013.
>
> I have known the author of *The Body Image Survival Guide* for a number of years. I recommend her book not because of a personal connection but because she offers solid, usable advice on body image issues. She also includes a chapter on boys' concerns with body image, a topic that is becoming better known but is still not discussed enough. Ms. Warhaft-Nadler also maintains a very active

presence on social media where she highlights current news and information about body image.

Websites

National Eating Disorders Association

https://www.nationaleatingdisorders.org/males-and-eating-disorders (US)

This URL leads to a page about males and eating disorders. It has several links to additional information, including research into disordered eating among boys and young men.

Gender Stereotypes

I recommended some of the older titles in my first book. They have stood the test of time, so I have included them here along with some newer resources.

Brown, Lyn Mikel et al. *Packaging Boyhood: Saving Our Sons from Superheroes, Slackers, and Other Media Stereotypes.* New York: St. Martins Press, 2009.

Packaging Boyhood offers a comprehensive look at male stereotypes in various media, including music, books, TV and film, and toy advertising. My copy of the book has at least 30 sticky notes protruding from the edges, marking all the valuable passages I have found through repeated readings.

Fine, Cordelia. *Delusions of Gender.* New York: W.W. Norton & Company, 2010.

Delusions of Gender debunks the myth that men's and women's brains are wired differently, instead naming culture as the primary agent in creating gender differences. Well researched and written with a sense of humour, this book is both informative and engaging. Note: Dr. Fine used an image I created in a 2014 presentation but my recommendation is not a quid pro quo. Her book is truly an excellent resource for anyone looking to understand how social forces shape ideas about gender.

Kindlon, Dan and Michael Thompson. *Raising Cain: Protecting the Emotional Life of Boys.* **New York: Random House, 2000.**

This book cautions parents not to fall into the trap of stunting their sons' emotional growth by toughening them with harsh discipline and lack of affection. It also advises parents not to accept an outmoded definition of manhood that focuses on physical strength, aggression, stoicism, and emotional distance.

Wiseman, Rosalind. *Masterminds and Wingmen: Helping Our Boys Cope with Schoolyard Power, Locker-Room Tests, Girlfriends, and the New Rules of Boy World.* **New York: Harmony Books, 2014.**

Ms. Wiseman discusses the social hierarchies that boys face in their daily lives and shows parents how to communicate effectively with their sons during their teenage years. Her book provides an excellent overview of boy culture and the challenges boys face growing up within that culture.

Media Literacy

There are dozens of media literacy resources available in print and online. I have highlighted only a few here but these provide a very good introduction to the topic as well as discussion of specific issues.

Books

As an aside, I'll note that I would also include *Packaging Boyhood*, from my Gender Stereotypes section, on this Media Literacy list. Many recent books I have come across deal specifically with girls and media literacy. The title I have included here deals with childhood in general.

Shewmaker, Jennifer. *Sexualized Media Messages and Our Children: Teaching Kids to be Smart Critics and Consumers.* Santa Barbara: Praeger, 2015.

Dr. Jennifer Shewmaker is a professor of psychology who has been writing for several years about media and gender. I know her personally and am a regular visitor to her blog. She offers an excellent discussion of how media affect children and provides advice to parents about how to help their children evaluate and critique media messages. Her chapter "The Family Matters," in particular, shows parents how much influence they have in their children's sexual socialization.

Websites

Common Sense Media

www.commonsensemedia.org (US)

Perhaps one of the better known media literacy sites, Common Sense Media is my go-to resource for reviews of films, TV shows, and video/online games. I would like to see more focus on gender representations in their reviews, but the site is comprehensive and easy to use: a green light on a certain age means the film, TV show, or game is appropriate for that age. A recent article highlighted films with "incredible role models for boys." The site is a good overall resource about current popular culture, and includes research into a wide range of topics of interest to parents, including a section on Parent Concerns that covers Sex, Gender, and Body Image.

CyberWise™

www.cyberwise.org (US)

CyberWise offers "online safety and education for parents and teachers." The site offers news, research and courses about digital and media literacy. It includes daily news updates and lots of articles in "learning hubs" like Cyberbullying, Digital Diet, Online Games, and various social media channels. CyberWise also provides online courses in new media, protecting privacy, and online reputation management, among others. Always current and very comprehensive, this site is a great resource for parents.

Jennifer Shewmaker

www.jennifershewmaker.com (US)

I included Dr. Shewmaker's book earlier in this section. Her blog is also a valuable resource and often includes series of posts about a particular topic, like building sexual self-efficacy, which she discussed in November and December of 2015.

Media Education Foundation

http://www.mediaed.org/ (US)

The Media Education Foundation is widely recognized for its excellent documentaries produced to "inspire critical thinking about the social, political, and cultural impact of American mass media." They have a robust section on gender, including several films that deal with representations of sexuality and masculinity. My research for this book includes a few of their films. Films are available for a small fee, but transcripts are provided for free. An excellent collection of thought-provoking materials.

MediaSmarts

www.mediasmarts.ca/ (Canada)

MediaSmarts is a Canadian non-profit organization that was established to promote digital and media literacy. Their website is designed for adults seeking to help children and teens develop strong digital and media literacy skills. The site's Research & Policy section includes a series of reports called *Young Canadians in a Wired World* which presents the results of the organization's 2013 survey of students in grades 4 to 11. MediaSmarts also offers some good introductory information on issues like gender representation and body image, both of which include sections on boys specifically. E-tutorials and workshops are also available, along with teacher resources searchable by grade. Like CyberWise, this site also includes a Daily News section.

Shaping Youth
www.shapingyouth.org. (US)

Shaping Youth is a non-profit organization dedicated to promoting media literacy and advocating for change among industry producers. I have known founder Amy Jussel for several years. Her blog posts offer in-depth discussion of many issues, including gender stereotypes, sexualization, and body image. Along with insightful commentary, Amy always includes valuable links to other resources in her posts.

Sexual Education for Teens

There are many books and websites available about puberty and sexual education for teens. I have listed a small sample below.

Books

The titles I have included here resonated with me personally, mainly because of their open and frank approach. You may want to read these before giving them to your teen, to be sure you are comfortable with the approach of each author.

Madaras, Lynda. *The "What's Happening to my Body?" Book for Boys.* 3rd revised ed. New York: William Morrow, 2012.

This book had me at the introduction, with its acknowledgement that "culture poses some rather tricky problems for young boys trying to find their way into manhood," followed by a description of the contrast between the tender side many boys have and the "conquering, tough-guy male sexuality" that dominates our culture. The author, a teacher of puberty and health education, covers male puberty in great detail and jumps right in with both feet—page 2 features images of four naked males, from early adolescence to adulthood, to demonstrate the physical changes that occur as the male body matures. Madaras aims for an audience of boys aged 9 to 15, but also suggests that parents read this book with their sons.

Madaras speaks from experience and shares many of the typical questions she hears in her classes. This book is comprehensive and includes very accurate diagrams to introduce readers to the male and female sex organs. It covers topics like: what is "normal" in the male sex organs; growth spurts and body types; physical changes outside of the sex organs; erections, ejaculation, and masturbation; and romantic and sexual feelings. There is also considerable emphasis on two very important messages: first, boys develop at different rates, and second, curiosity about sex is normal and healthy. Because the focus is on puberty, little is said about STIs and safe sex.

Harris, Robie H. *It's Perfectly Normal: Changing Bodies, Growing Up, Sex, and Sexual Health.* **3r. ed. Somerville, MA: Candlewick Press, 2009.**

It's Perfectly Normal uses a picture book format to discuss puberty with kids. Bird and bee characters appear throughout the book with sidebar comments. I found the approach a little juvenile, especially the animation, but it might work with some children. The book is not aimed at boys specifically but is very informative and contains a good deal of information about STIs and condoms. It also broaches the subject of abortion. Because it relies on animation, the illustrations are less accurate than the Madaras book listed above, but overall the information is presented clearly. (A new 20th anniversary edition was released in late 2014.)

Hasler, Nikol. *Sex: A Book for Teens.* **San Francisco: Zest Books, 2010.**

Have you heard of the online comedy series *The Midwest Teen Sex Show*? I hadn't but I did see this book, written by its host, on a list of recommended sex ed books. It might be a tad shocking for parents but it approaches the topic of sex in a manner that many teens might like. Written for readers aged 15 and up, the book answers some very tricky but legitimate questions in forthright language while keeping the tone light—even when talking about anal sex. On that topic, Hasler offers very clear advice: don't do it if you feel pressured, it is more complicated and requires more preparation than oral or vaginal, and always use condoms and a lubricant. After a full discussion of the preparation side of things, she uses her typical frank language to describe why people like anal: "Our bodies have different hot spots, and for some that hot spot is in the butt." Hasler also includes very detailed sections on STIs, birth control, and pregnancy.

I quite liked this book as a guide for teens but please know that it is not for everyone. The cover illustration may even be too much, as it features, in the author's words, "two cows humping." Hasler is very open about anal sex and stimulation, kinks, and fetishes (acknowledging that BDSM is not appropriate for teens). She also offers tips for masturbation and even advice on how a teen can buy a vibrator. Her final chapter on communication is a good one, and gives a few tips on what a teen should do if he can't talk to his parents about sex.

If you are considering this book for your teen, read it first to ensure it suits your values and vision for sexual education. (As of the time of writing, *Sex: A Book for Teens* was only available in electronic format, although I was able to borrow a paperback version from my local library.)

Websites

The list I've included here is far from exhaustive. For websites I have focused mainly on North American sources, but have not included the many organizations that operate at state and provincial levels. To find more, search "sex ed for teens" in your preferred search engine, and add a geographic locator to narrow the search if necessary. The sites below are comprehensive and written for teens in language that is clear, non-judgmental, and accessible.

Go Ask Alice

http://goaskalice.columbia.edu/ (US)

Go Ask Alice is a health promotion website affiliated with Columbia University. The Q&A Library includes a "Sexual and Reproductive Health" section. Go Ask Alice offers "reliable, accurate, accessible, culturally competent information." The answers are well-written, occasionally witty, and always informative, often including links to additional resources. Nothing seems to be off-limits: there are categories for sexual variety, sexual secretions, erotica and pornography, and fetishes and philias. The site is visited by people of all ages, including college and high school students.

It's Your Sex Life

http://www.itsyoursexlife.com/ (US)

Although a product of MTV, this site is supported by reputable organizations like Planned Parenthood, The National Coalition for Sexual Health, and the Kaiser Family Foundation. Designed to appeal to teens, the site includes celebrities and several links to MTV programming but also many online and social media resources about pregnancy prevention, STIs, relationships, and LGBTQ. The "Hotlines and Resources" list is quite extensive and a parallel campaign called "GYT (Get Yourself Tested)" aims to raise awareness of STIs and position testing as "an act of pride, not shame."

PlanetAhead

http://www.planetahead.ca/ (Canada)

The animated characters Condom Man and Lucy Lubricant add little to this site, but the site itself is a good resource for teens. Unlike other sites I've listed here, PlanetAhead comes not from a large national organization but from the Vancouver Coastal Health Authority. There are no bells and whistles, but concise bits of information—quick and dirty, if you will. The "Under Pressure" menu is especially strong, covering sexual orientation, relationships, how to know when you are ready for sex, and consent. This site also includes great FAQs in its resources section, featuring several questions from readers of the site.

Planned Parenthood

http://www.plannedparenthood.org/teens (This site is American but the organization has global reach and local chapters in major cities.)

Planned Parenthood is a well known global organization. Through their website and reports they offer detailed sexual education. Planned Parenthood also provides direct care through various health centres. The website highlighted above is directed at teens and covers a wide range of sexual health issues in its Learn menu.

Scarleteen

http://www.scarleteen.com/ (US-based but with a global audience)

Scarleteen is perhaps the best known online sexual health resource for teens. Operating since 1998, the site offers articles, guides and fact sheets written by adults and teens. Scarleteen also provides direct services to answer teens' questions, including message boards, text services, live chat, and advice columns.

Sex, etc.

http://sexetc.org/ (US)

Billed as "by teens" and "for teens," this site is very easy to navigate. It includes videos, FAQs, and a forum for teens to ask questions. The Action Center is another interesting addition, offering a clinic finder, a tool for starting communication about sex with a parent or partner, and options for teens to get active on sexual health issues. An interactive map of the United States outlines how states handle sexual health issues like sexual education, LGBTQ rights, and emergency contraception. The site is published by Answer (http://answer.rutgers.edu/), a "national organization that provides and promotes unfettered access to comprehensive sexuality education" affiliated with Rutgers University. There is also a print magazine available.

SexualityandU.ca

http://www.sexualityandu.ca/ (Canada)

Created by the Society of Obstetricians and Gynecologists (SOGS), this site is not teen-specific and lacks the teen-friendly aesthetic of Scarleteen and Sex etc., but I have included it because of the depth of topics covered. It includes basic physical health, puberty, sexual assault, masturbation, and sexual diversity. In addition to textual information, the site includes FAQs that might be of value to parents and teens.

Teen Health Source

http://teenhealthsource.com/ (Canada)

Teen Health Source is a sexual health information service run by teens. Created by Planned Parenthood Toronto, the site provides teens with written resources on sexual health topics, as well as a peer education service that puts teens aged 13-19 in touch with trained volunteers of a similar age. Teens can contact volunteers via text, email, phone, and website chat.

Sex Ed Research

For parents in the US who may want to make a case for broader sexual education in their children's school, this site contains some valuable information.

Future of Sex Education (FoSE)

http://www.futureofsexed.org/youthhealthrights.html (US)

The purpose of FoSE is "to create a national dialogue about the future of sex education and to promote the institutionalization of comprehensive sexuality education in public schools." The organization's website contains many resources and facts about the current state of sex education in the US.

Sexual Aggression, Harassment, and Consent

It is surprisingly difficult to find books and online resources geared toward teens that deal with sexual aggression and consent. Much of the material I came across discussed the sexual abuse of boys, not peer-on-peer assault or harassment. Although limited in number, the resources below contain valuable information.

Websites

Driver's Ed for the Sexual Super Highway: Navigating Consent

http://www.scarleteen.com/article/abuse_assault/drivers_ed_for_the_sexual_superhighway_navigating_consent (US)

I referenced Scarleteen above, but wanted to highlight this specific article about consent. It is long and well worth printing for teens to read. Along with a clear definition of consent, it lays out the rules of consent, the importance of using words to communicate consent, and accepting and respecting nonconsent.

Kids Help Phone Info Booth

http://www.kidshelpphone.ca/Teens/InfoBooth.aspx (Canada)

The Info Booth page from Kids Help Phone provides answers to myriad issues of concern to children and teens. There is a specific section on violence and abuse that covers sexual abuse, harassment, and assault, as well as dating violence. Each topic page defines the issue and offers strategies on how to handle it. Kids Help Phone also provides online forums for teens to discuss the problems they are facing, and a toll-free number to access free, anonymous counselling.

RAINN

https://rainn.org/get-information/types-of-sexual-assault/male-sexual-assault (US)

The Rape, Abuse & Incest National Network (RAINN) provides an overview of how sexual assault can affect male victims and also offers confidential online chat services and support for men and boys.

About the Author

Crystal Smith is the author of *The Achilles Effect: What Pop Culture is Teaching Young Boys about Masculinity*. Through her *Achilles Effect* blog (www.achilleseffect.com) and social media channels, Crystal discusses current depictions of masculinity in popular culture and their potential impact on boys. Her work has been covered in *The Boston Globe*, *Advertising Age*, and *Feministing*, and she has appeared on *HuffPost Live* and *The Roy Green Show*. She lives in Oakville, Ontario with her husband and two children.

Bibliography

Books

American Psychological Association, Task Force on the Sexualization of Girls. (2010).*Report of the APA Task Force on the Sexualization of Girls.* http://www.apa.org/pi/women/programs/girls/report-full.pdf.

Bordo, Susan. *The Male Body: A New Look at Men in Public and in Private.* New York: Farrar, Straus and Giroux.1999.

Brown, Lyn Mikel et al. *Packaging Boyhood: Saving our Sons from Superheroes, Slackers, and Other Media Stereotypes.* New York: St. Martin's Press, 2009.

Coy, Maddy et al. *'Sex without consent, I suppose that is rape': How young people in England understand sexual consent.* London: Office of the Children's Commissioner, 2013.

Day, Lori and Charlotte Kugler. *Her Next Chapter: How Mother-Daughter Book Clubs Can Help Girls Navigate Malicious Media, Risky Relationships, Girl Gossip, and So Much More.* Chicago: Chicago Review Press, 2014.

Dines, Gail. *Pornland: How Porn Has Hijacked Our Sexuality.* Boston: Beacon Press, 2010.

Hill, Catherine and Holly Kearl. *Crossing the Line: Sexual Harassment at School.* Washington: AAUW, 2011.

Holland, Jack. *Misogyny: The World's Oldest Prejudice.* New York: Carroll & Graf, 2006.

Kimmel, Michael et al. (eds). *Cultural Encyclopedia of the Penis.* Lanham, MD: Rowman & Littlefield, 2014.

Kunkel, Dale et al. *Sex on TV 4.* Menlo Park: Kaiser Family Foundation, 2005.

Madaras, Lynda. *The "What's Happening to My Body?" Book for Boys.* New York: HarperCollins, 2007.

Marsiglio,W., Ries, A., Sonenstein, F., Troccoli, K. & Whitehead,W. *It's a Guy*

Thing: Boys, Young Men, and Teen Pregnancy Prevention. Washington, DC: National Campaign to Prevent Teen, 2006.

Milestone, Katie and Anneke Meyer. *Gender & Popular Culture.* Cambridge, UK: Polity Press, 2012.

Myers, D.G. *Social Psychology.* 11th ed. New York: McGraw-Hill, 2012

Pope, Harrison G. et al. *The Adonis Complex: How to Identify, Treat, and Prevent Body Obsession in Men and Boys.* New York: Touchstone, 2000.

Toulalan, Sarah. *Imagining Sex: Pornography and Bodies in Seventeenth-Century England.* Oxford: Oxford University Press, 2007. Kindle Edition.

Valenti, Jessica. *The Purity Myth: How America's Obsession with Virginity is Hurting Young Women.* Berkeley: Seal Press, 2009.

Wardy, Melissa Atkins. *Redefining Girly: How Parents Can Fight the Stereotyping and Sexualizing of Girlhood, From Birth to Tween.* Chicago: Chicago Review Press, 2014.

Films

Keith, Thomas. *The Bro Code: How Contemporary Culture Creates Sexist Men* Transcript. Northampton, MA: Media Education Foundation, 2011.

Jhally, Sut. *Dreamworlds 3: Desire, Sex and Power in Music Video* Transcript. Northampton, MA: Media Education Foundation, 2007.

Jhally, Sut. *Asking For It: The Ethics & Erotics of Sexual Consent.* Transcript. Media Education Foundation. 2010.

Journal Articles

Alexander, Susan M. "Stylish Hard Bodies: Branded Masculinity in *Men's Health* Magazine." *Sociological Perspectives* 46, no.4 (2003).

Arnett, Jeffrey Jensen. "The Sounds of Sex: Sex in Teens' Music and Music Videos" *Sexual Teens, Sexual Media: Investigating Media's Influence on Adolescent Sexuality*. Jane D. Brown et al, eds. Mahwah, NJ: Lawrence Erlbaum Associates, 2002.

Attwood, Feona. "'Tits and ass and porn and fighting': Male heterosexuality in magazines for men" *International Journal of Cultural Studies* 8, no. 1 (2005).

Attwood, Feona. "Sexed Up: Theorizing the Sexualization of Culture" *Sexualities* 9, no. 1 (2006).

Ayala, Jessica et al. *Promoting Sexual Health for Young Men*. Calgary: Calgary Sexual Health Centre, 2008.

Botta, Renée. "For Your Health? The Relationship Between Magazine Reading and Adolescents' Body Image and Eating Disturbances" *Sex Roles* 48, no. 9/10 (2003).

Boyce, William et al. "Sexual Health of Canadian Youth: Findings from the *Canadian Youth, Sexual Health, and HIV/AIDS Study*" *Canadian Journal of Human Sexuality*, 15, no. 2 (2006).

Boynton, Petra. "Better dicks through drugs? The penis as pharmaceutical target." *Scan: Journal of Media Arts and Culture* 1, no. 3 (2004).

Braun-Courville, D.K. and Mary Rojas. "Exposure to Sexually Explicit Web Sites and Adolescent Sexual Attitudes and Behaviours." *Journal of Adolescent Health* 45, no.2 (2009).

Bridges, AJ et al. "Aggression and sexual behavior in best-selling pornography videos: a content analysis update" *Violence Against Women* 16, no. 10 (2010).

Brown, Jane D. and Kelly L'Engle. "X-Rated: Sexual Attitudes and Behaviors Associated with U.S. Early Adolescents' Exposure to Sexually Explicit Media." *Communication Research* 36, no. 1, (2009).

Caminis, Argyro et al. "Psychosocial predictors or sexual initiation and high-risk sexual behaviors in early adolescence" *Child and Adolescent Psychiatry and Mental Health* 1, no. 14. (2007).

Carroll, Jason S. "Generation XXX: Pornography Acceptance and Use Among Emerging Adults." *Journal of Adolescent Research* 23, no. 1 (2008).

Claxton, Shannon E. and Manfred H. M. van Dulmen. "Casual Sexual Relationships and Experiences in Emerging Adulthood" *Emerging Adulthood* 1, no. 2 (2013).

Collier, Katie et al. "Homophobic Name-Calling Among Secondary School Students and Its Implications for Mental Health" *Journal of Youth and Adolescence* 42, no. 3 (2013).

Collins, RL et al. "Entertainment television as healthy sex educator: the impact of condom-efficacy information in an episode of Friends" *Pediatrics* 112, no. 5 (2003).

Coy, Maddy and Miranda A.H. Horvath. "'Lads' Mags', Young Men's Attitudes towards Women and Acceptance of Myths about Sexual Aggression." *Feminism & Psychology*. 20, no. 2 (2010).

Davies, Michelle. "Male sexual assault victims: a selective review of the literature and implications for support services" *Aggression and Violent Behavior*, 7, no. 3 (2002).

Dill, Karen E. et al. "Effects of exposure to sex-stereotyped video game characters on tolerance of sexual harassment." *Journal of Experimental Social Psychology* 44, no.5 (2008).

Donaldson, Abigail et al. "Receipt of Sexual Health Information From Parents, Teachers, and Healthcare Providers by Sexually Experienced US Adolescents" *Journal of Adolescent Health* 53, no. 2 (2013).

Eisenberg Marla E. et al. "Muscle-enhancing Behaviours Among Adolescent Girls and Boys" *Pediatrics* 130, no. 6 (2012).

Eyal, Keren and Keli Finnerty. "The Portrayal of Sexual Intercourse on Television: How, Who, and With What Consequences?" *Mass Communication and Society*. 12, no. 2, (2009).

Farrar, Kirstie M. "Sexual Intercourse on Television: Do Safe Sex Messages Matter?" *Journal of Broadcasting & Electronic Media* 50, no. 4 (2006).

Field, Alison et al. "Prospective Associations of Concerns about Physique and the Development of Obesity, Binge Drinking, and Drug Use Among Adolescent Boys and Young Adult Men." *JAMA Pediatrics* 168, no. 1; (2014).

Fisher, Deborah A. et al "Televised sexual content and parental mediation: Influences on adolescent sexuality" *Media Psychology* 12, no. 2 (2009).

Fisher, Nicola L. and Afroditi Pina. "An overview of the literature on female-perpetrated adult male sexual victimization" *Aggression and Violent Behavior*, 18, no. 1 (2013).

Flood, Michael. "The Harms of Pornography Exposure Among Children and Young People." *Child Abuse Review* 18, no. 6 (2009).

Foubert, John D. "Pornography Viewing among Fraternity Men: Effects on Bystander Intervention, Rape Myth Acceptance and Behavioral Intent to Commit Sexual Assault" *Sexual Addiction and Compulsivity*. 18, no. 4 (2011).

Fredrickson, Barbara L. and Tomi-Ann Roberts. "Objectification Theory: Toward Understanding Women's Lived Experiences and Mental Health Risks" *Psychology of Women Quarterly* 21, no.2 (1997).

Frisen, Ann and Kristina Holmqvist. "Physical, Sociocultural, and Behavioral Factors Associated with Body-Esteem in 16-Year-Old Swedish Boys and Girls" *Sex Roles* 63, no.5-6 (2010).

Funk, Leah C. and Cherie D. Werhun. "'You're Such a Girl!' The Psychological Drain of the Gender-Role Harassment of Men" *Sex Roles* 65, no. 1-2 (2011).

Galdi, Silvia et al. "Objectifying Media: Their Effect on Gender Role Norms and Sexual Harassment of Women." *Psychology of Women Quarterly* 38, no. 3 (2014).

Gill, Rosalind et al. "Body Projects and the Regulation of Normative Masculinity" *Body & Society* 11, no. 1 (2005).

Gill, Rosalind. "Media, Empowerment and the 'Sexualization of Culture' Debates" *Sex Roles* 66, no. 11-12 (2012).

Giordano, Peggy et al. "Gender and the Meanings of Adolescent Romantic Relationships: A Focus on Boys" *American Sociological Review* 71, no. 2 (2006).

Gruber, James E. and Susan Fineran. "Comparing the Impact of Bullying and Sexual Harassment Victimization on the Mental and Physical Health of Adolescents" *Sex Roles* 59, no 1-2. (2008).

Gunasekera, Hasantha et al. "Sex and drugs in popular movies: an analysis of the top 200 films." *Journal of the Royal Society of Medicine* 98, no. 10 (2005).

Halpern-Felsher, Bonnie et al. "Oral Versus Vaginal Sex Among Adolescents: Perceptions, Attitudes, and Behavior." *Pediatrics* 115, no. 4 (2005).

Hampton, Mary Rucklos et al."Influence of Teens' Perceptions of Parental Disapproval and Peer Behaviour on Their Initiation of Sexual Intercourse" *The Canadian Journal of Human Sexuality*. 14, no. 3-4 (2005).

Hatoum, Ida Jodette and Deborah Belle. "Mags and Abs: Media Consumption and Bodily Concerns in Men" *Sex Roles* 51, no. 7/8 (2004).

Heldman, Caroline and Lisa Wade. "Hook-Up Culture: Setting a New Research Agenda" *Sexuality Research and Social Policy*. 7, no. 4 (2010).

Horvath, Miranda H. et al. "'Lights on at the end of the party': Are lads' mags mainstreaming dangerous sexism?" *British Journal of Psychology*. 103, no. 4 (2012).

Huang, David Y. C. "Parental Monitoring During Early Adolescence Deters Adolescent Sexual Initiation: Discrete-Time Survival Mixture Analysis" *Journal of Child and Family Studies*. 20, no. 4. (2011).

Huesmann, L. Rowell. "An Information Processing Model for the Development of Aggression" *Aggressive Behavior* 4, no. 1 (1988)

Humphreys. Terry. "Understanding Sexual Consent: An Empirical Investigation of the Normative Script for Young Heterosexual Adults" in *Making Sense of Sexual Consent* Mark Cowling, Paul Reynolds, eds., Surrey, UK: Ashgate, 2004.

Hust, Stacy et al. "Establishing and adhering to sexual consent: The association of reading magazines and college students' sexual consent negotiation." *Journal of Sex Research* 51, no. 3 (2014).

Jones, Diana Carlson and Joy K. Crawford. "The Peer Appearance Culture During Adolescence: Gender and Body Mass Variations." *Journal of Youth and Adolescence* 35, no. 2 (2006).

Jozkowski, Kristen N. et al. "Consenting to Sexual Activity: The Development and Psychometric Assessment of Dual Measures of Consent" *Archives of Sexual Behaviour* 43, no. 3 (2014), p. 438.
Humphreys, Terry and Ed Herold. "Sexual Consent in Heterosexual Relationships: Development of a New Measure" *Sex Roles* 57, no. 3 (2007).

Kaestle, Christine et al. "Young Age at First Sexual Intercourse and Sexually Transmitted Infections in Adolescents and Young Adults" *American Journal of Epidemiology* 161, no. 8 (2005).

Kim, Janna et al. "From Sex to Sexuality: Exposing the Heterosexual Script on Primetime Network Television" *Journal of Sex Research* 44, no. 2 (2007).

Krassas, Nicole et al. "'Master Your Johnson': Sexual Rhetoric in *Maxim* and *Stuff* Magazines" *Sexuality & Culture* 7, no. 3. (2003).

Lawler, Margaret and Elizabeth Nixon. "Body Dissatisfaction Among Adolescent Boys and Girls: The Effects of Body Mass, Peer Appearance Culture and Internalization of Body Ideals" *Journal of Youth and Adolescence.* 40, no. 1 (2011).

Lerum, Kari and Shari L. Dworkin. "'Bad Girls Rule': An Interdisciplinary Feminist Commentary on the Report of the APA Task Force on the Sexualization of Girls" *Journal of Sex Research.* 46, no.4 (2009).

Levant, Ronald F. "Men and Masculinity," in Vol. 2 of *Encyclopedia of Women and Gender: Sex Similarities and Differences and the Impact of Society on Gender.* ed. Judith Worrell. (San Diego: Academic Press, 2001).

Lever, Janet et al. "Does Size Matter? Men's and Women's Views on Penis Size Across the Lifespan" *Psychology of Men & Masculinity* 7, no. 3 (2006.

Littleton, Heather et al. "Priming of Consensual and Nonconsensual Sexual Scripts: An Experimental Test of the Role of Scripts in Rape Attributions" *Sex Roles* 54, no. 7-8 (2006).

Löfgren-Mårtenson, Lotta and Sven-Axel Månsson. "Lust, Love, and Life: A Qualitative Study of Swedish Adolescents' Perceptions and Experiences with Pornography" *Journal of Sex Research.* 47, no. 6 (2010).

Luder, Marie-Thérèse et al. "Associations Between Online Pornography and Sexual Behavior Among Adolescents: Myth or Reality?" *Archives of Sexual Behavior* 40, no. 5 (2011).

Maddison, Stephen. "The Biopolitics of the Penis" *Cultural Studies Now* Conference, 2007. http://culturalstudiesresearch.org/wp-content/uploads/2012/10/MaddisonBiopoliticsPenis.pdf.

Marcell, Arik A. et al. "Male Adolescent Sexual and Reproductive Health Care" *Pediatrics* 128, no. 6 (2011).

Martino, Steven et al. "Exposure to Degrading Versus Nondegrading Music Lyrics and Sexual Behavior Among Youth. *Pediatrics* 118, no. 2 (2006).

Maxwell, Christopher D. et al. "The Nature and Predictors of Sexual Victimization and Offending Among Adolescents" *Journal of Youth and Adolescence* 32, no. 6 (2003).

Maxwell, Kimberly A. "Friends: The Role of Peer Influence Across Adolescent Risk Behaviors" *Journal of Youth and Adolescence.* 31, no. 4 (2002).

McMahon, Sarah and Lawrence G. Farmer. "An Updated Measure for Assessing Subtle Rape Myths" *Social Work Research* 35, no. 2 (2011).

Morrison, T.G. et al. "Correlates of genital perceptions among Canadian post-secondary students." *Electronic Journal of Human Sexuality.* 8 (2005).

National Campaign to Prevent Teen Pregnancy. "Parent-Child Communication About Sex and Related Topics" *Science Says* no. 25 (May 2006).

Oderda, Marco and Paolo Gontero. "Non-invasive methods of penile lengthening: fact or fiction?" *BJU International* 107, no. 8 (2011).

Ott, Mary A. "Examining the Development and Sexual Behavior of Adolescent Males" *Journal of Adolescent Health* 46, no. 4, Supplement (2010).

Owens, Eric W. et al. "The Impact of Internet Pornography on Adolescents: A Review of the Research" *Sexual Addiction and Compulsivity* 19, no 1-2 (2012).

Papadaki, Evangelia (Lina), "Feminist Perspectives on Objectification", *The Stanford Encyclopedia of Philosophy (Winter 2012 Edition)*, Edward N. Zalta (ed.), http://plato.stanford.edu/archives/win2012/entries/feminism-objectification/.

Peter, Jochen and Patti M. Valkenburg. "Adolescents' Exposure to Sexually Explicit Internet Material and Sexual Preoccupancy: A Three-Wave Panel Study." *Media Psychology* 11, no. 2 : 2008.

Peter, Jochen and Patti M. Valkenburg. "Processes Underlying the Effects of Adolescents' Use of Sexually Explicit Internet Material: The Role of Perceived Realism" *Communication Research* 37, no. 3: 2010.

Petrie, Trent A. et al. "Biopsychosocial and Physical Correlates of Middle School Boys' and Girls' Body Satisfaction." *Sex Roles* 63, no. 9-10 (2010).

Price, Myeshia N. And Janet Shibley Hyde. "When Two Isn't Better Than One: Predictors of Early Sexual Activity in Adolescence Using a Cumulative Risk Model" *Journal of Youth and Adolescence* 38, no. 8 (2009).

Primack, Brian A. et al. "Exposure to Sexual Lyrics and Sexual Experience Among Urban Adolescents" *American Journal of Preventive Medicine* 36, no. 4 (2009).

Ricciardelli, Lina A. et al. "A Longitudinal Investigation of the Development of Weight and Muscle Concerns Among Preadolescent Boys." *Journal of Youth and Adolescence* 35, no. 2 (2006).

Ricciardelli, Rosemary. "Investigating Hegemonic Masculinity: Portrayals of Masculinity in Men's Lifestyle Magazines" *Sex Roles* 63, no. 1 (2010).

Ringrose, Jessica et al. *A qualitative study of children, young people and 'sexting': a report prepared for the NSPCC* London: National Society for the Prevention of Cruelty to Children, 2012.

Ryan, Kathryn. "The Relationship between Rape Myths and Sexual Scripts: The Social Construction of Rape" *Sex Roles* 65, no. 11-12 (2011).

Sabina, Chiara et al. "The Nature and Dynamics of Internet Pornography Exposure for Youth." *CyberPsychology & Behavior* 11, no. 6 (2008).

Shamloul, Rany. "Treatment of Men Complaining of Short Penis" *Urology* 65, no. 6 (2005).

Slater, Amy and Marika Tiggemann. "Body Image and Distorted Eating in Adolescent Girls and Boys: A Test of Objectification Theory." *Sex Roles* 63, no. 1-2 (2010)

Smith, Marshall. "Youth Viewing Sexually Explicit Material Online: Addressing the Elephant on the Screen" *Sexuality Research and Social Policy*. 10, no.1 (2013).

Smolak, Linda and Jonathan A. Stein. "A Longitudinal Investigation of Gender Role and Muscle Building in Adolescent Boys" *Sex Roles* 63, no. 9-10 (2010).

Stern, Susannah and Jane D. Brown. "From Twin Beds to Sex at Your Fingertips: Teen Sexuality in Movies, Music, Television, and the Internet, 1950 to 2005 in *Changing Portrayal of Adolescents in Media Since 1950*. London: Oxford University Press (2008).

Taylor, Laramie D. "All for Him: Articles About Sex in American Lad Magazines" *Sex Roles* 52, no. 3-4, (2005).

Thompson, Kevin J. et al. "The Sociocultural Attitudes Towards Appearance Scale-2 (SATAQ): Development and Validation." *International Journal of Eating Disorders* 35, no. 3 (2004).

Tiggeman, Marika. "Television and Adolescent Body Image: The Role of Program Content and Viewing Motivation" *Journal of Social and Clinical Psychology*. 24, no. 3 (2005).

Tolman, Deborah et al. "Rethinking the Associations between Television Viewing and Adolescent Sexuality Development: Bringing Gender into Focus" *Journal of Adolescent Health* 40, no. 1 (2007).

Udell, Wadiya et al. "The Relationship Between Early Sexual Debut and Psychosocial Outcomes: A Longitudinal Study of Dutch Adolescents" *Archives of Sexual Behavior* 39, no. 5 (2010).

Weber, Mathias et al. "Peers, Parents and Pornography: Exploring Adolescents' Exposure to Sexually Explicit Material and Its Developmental Correlates" *Sexuality & Culture* 16, no. 4 (2012).

Westwood, Michael and Jorge Pinzon. "Adolescent male health." *Paediatric Child Health* 13, no. 1 (2008).

Wiederman, Michael. "The Gendered Nature of Sexual Scripts" *The Family Journal* 13, no. 4 (2005).

Wright, Paul J. et al. "Research on Sex in the Media: What Do We Know About Effects on Children and Adolescents" in *Handbook of Children and the Media*. 2nd ed. Dorothy G. Singer and Jerome L. Singer, eds, Los Angeles: Sage Publications, 2012.

Wylie, Kevan R. and Ian Eardley. "Penile size and the 'small penis syndrome.'" *BJUI* 99, no. 6 (2007).

Young, Amy et al. "Adolescents' Experience of Sexual Assault by Peers: Prevalence and Nature of Victimization Occurring Within and Outside School" *Journal of Youth and Adolescence* 38, no. 8 (2009).

Zhang, Yuanyuan et al. "The Relationship Between Exposure to Sexual Music Videos and Young Adults' Sexual Attitudes" *Journal of Broadcasting & Electronic Media* 52, no. 3 (2008).

Zilbergeld, Bernard as quoted in McKee, Alan. "Does size matter? Dominant discourses about penises in Western Culture." *Cultural Studies Review* 10, no. 2: (2004).

Index

1 is 2 Many, 61
2 Chainz, 68
50 Cent, 68
679, 66
A$AP Rocky, 68
Adonis Complex, The, 133
aggression
  and masculinity, 135
American Apparel, 16
anal sex. *See* sexual activity
Anaconda, 99
Animal Ambition, 68
Animals, 78
Antidote, 67
Are You the One, 56
Arrow, 33, 89
Asking For It: The Ethics & Erotics of Consensual Sex, 120
Atlas, Charles, 88
Beckham, David, 17, 87
Below Deck, 39, 57
Beyoncé, 67
Bieber, Justin, 90, 125
birth control. *See* contraception
Blurred Lines, 58, 66, 99
body esteem
  for bigger boys, 128–29
  for smaller boys, 127–28
body image, 87
  advice for parents, 125–29
  and pubertal development, 95
  and sexual satisfaction, 88, 91
  internalization of body ideals, 93–95
  male, 133
  muscle-enhancing behaviours, 92
  peer influence, 94–95, 96
Bordo, Susan, 88
Boynton, Petra, 87, 96, 99
bro code, 76, 82, 85, 110, 123, 124
Brown, Lyn Mikel, 107, 134
Buckwild, 42
bystander effect, 76–77
  and pornography, 76
Carl's Jr., 17, 109
casual sex
  consequences, in media portrayals, 42–43
  media portrayals of, 39–40, 42
Cavill, Henry, 90
chlamydia, 45
Common Sense Media, 136
condoms
  and hookups, 42–44
  impact of media on use, 43
  impact of pornography on use, 46
  rates of use among boys, 45–47
  reasons for non-use, 46
  STI and pregnancy prevention, 44–47
consent, 53–62
  and alcohol, 56, 121, 124
  communication of, 55–56
  education, 57, 62
  impact of sex role stereotypes, 55, 56
  media portrayals of, 58–60
  role of parents in teaching,

119–22
contraception, 47
    boys' role, 118
    early sexual debut, 47
Coy, Maddy, 54, 57, 61, 70
Crawford, Joy K., 94, 95, 96
Cultural Encyclopedia of the Penis, 96
CyberWise, 136
Cyrus, Miley, 67
Daredevil, 90
Day, Lori, 104, 109, 112, 114
Delusions of Gender, 134
Derulo, Jason, 3, 109, 125
Dines, Gail, 24, 26, 71
Don Jon, 13
Drake, 67, 68, 125
Driver's Ed for the Sexual Super Highway, 145
early sexual debut. *See* sexual activity
Eisenberg, Marla, 92
ESPN Magazine, 93
F**kin Problems, 68
Family Guy, 75, 76, 86, 131
Fanny Hill, 20, 96
femininity, 10
Fetty Wap, 66, 67
FHM, 57, 66, 69
FHRITP, 122
Fine, Cordelia, 134
Fire Emblem: Awakening, 64
Fisher, Deborah, 103, 105, 108
Flo Rida, 66, 99
Flood, Michael, 23, 30
Foubert, John D., 26, 76
Future of Sex Education (FoSE), 144

GDFR, 99
gender stereotypes, 10–12, 18, 111
    and communication, 106
    and sexual aggression, 81
    body image, 12
    effect on relationships, 11
    in children's play, 11
    in heterosexual script, 12
Gill, Rosalind, 88, 96
Go Ask Alice, 141
Goffman, Erving, 15, 64
Gomez, Selena, 67
gonorrhea, 45
Grande, Ariana, 67
H&M, 17
Harper, Bryce, 93
Harris, Robie H, 139
Hasler, Nikol, 140
heterosexual script, 12–15, 18, 78
HIV, 45
hookup culture, 39–43
    and alcohol, 41
    and condom use, 41
Hooters, 17
Hotline Bling, 67
Humphreys, Terry, 54, 60
Hustler, 25, 26, 69
I Love Ugly, 16
I Modi, 20
intimacy. *See* relationships
Iron Man 3, 65
It's On Us, 61
It's Perfectly Normal: Changing Bodies, Growing Up, Sex, and Sexual Health, 139
It's Your Sex Life, 141

Jay-Z, 67
Jhally, Sut, 63
Jonas, Nick, 91, 125
Jones, Diana Carlson, 94, 95, 96
Juliette, 21
Katz, Jackson, 70
Kids HelpPhone Info Booth, 145
Kimmel, Michael, 96
Kindlon, Dan, 135
Klein, Calvin, 87, 88, 90
Krassas, Nicole, 57, 66
lad magazines, 65, 69, 99
    degradging content, 70–71
Lamar, Kendrick, 68
Lever, Janet, 98
Lil Wayne, 67
Love Me, 67
Madaras, Lynda, 138
Maddison, Stephen, 97
Magic Mike XXL, 90
Marcell, Arik, 37, 38, 45
Maroon 5, 78
Marquis de Sade, 20
masculinity, 5, 10
    and aggression, 49
    and body image, 96
    and boys' relationships, 49
    and homophobia, 82
    and sexual experience, 14, 38, 55, 61
    body ideal, 95
Masterminds and Wingmen, 135
Maxim, 66
Media Education Foundation, 137
MediaSmarts, 137
Men's Fitness, 91, 100

Men's Health, 91, 99, 100
Mendes, Shawn, 125
Minaj, Nicki, 99
music videos
    and sexual objectification, 66
    degrading lyrics, images, 67–68
    popularity with teens, 68
My House, 66
National Eating Disorders Association, 134
NFL, 65
No Medicore, 99
No Mediocre, 68
Nuts, 66
oral sex. *See* sexual activity
Packaging Boyhood, 108, 134, 135
parents
    activism, 130–31
    and boys' sexual health, 118
    avoiding stereotypes, 111
    communication with boys, 105–7
    discussing pornography with kids, 114–17
    helping boys affected by sexual aggression, 124–25
    helping boys with sexual anxiety, 129–30
    mediation of TV viewing, 108
    monitoring peer relationships, 110
    preventing early sexual debut, 48
    role in boys' sexual socialization, 105
    role in sexual education, 117–19

teaching boys about sexual aggression, 123–25
teaching boys body esteem, 125–29
teaching consent, 119–22
teaching media literacy, 107–10
Party Down South, 39
peers, 38, 50
    role in sexual socialization, 110–11
penis size, 96–98
    ads for performance enhancement, **99**
    and pornography, 97, 100
    in media, 98–99
    in men's magazines, 100
Penthouse, 25
Peter, Jochen, 28, 29, 117
Pinzon, Jorge, 100, 119, 129
PlanetAhead, 142
Planned Parenthood, 142
Playboy, 25, 66
Pope, Harrison, 133
Pornland, 24, 71
pornography, 19
    and consent, 30
    and sexual aggression, 115
    and sexual anxiety. *See* penis size
    as sexual educator, 24, 28, 29, 38
    attitudes toward casual sex, 29
    depiction of men, 27
    discussing with kids, 114–17
    free online sites, 25
    gonzo, 26, 71
    impact on boys, 27
    in history, 19
    perceived realism, 29, 30, 115
    reasons for use, 23–24
    sexual violence in, 25–27
    usage among teens, 22–23
pregnancy
    rates among teens, 47
RAINN, 145
Raising Cain, 135
rape
    jokes, 75
    male rape myth, 83
    myths, 72–77, 84
    Sayreville, NJ, 81
    Steubenville, OH, 73
Real World, 90
Redefining Girly, 109, 130
relationships
    boys and intimacy, 49–50
    communication, 50
Ricciardelli, Lina, 94, 95
Ricciardelli, Rosemary, 91
Ryan, Kathryn, 67
safe sex messages
    in media, 42–44
Scarleteen, 143
Scott, Travis, 67
sex
    and alcohol, in media, 56–57
Sex for Guys, 116
sex role stereotypes, 78, 111
    and boys' relationships, 49–51
    and consent, 55, 56, 61
    and sexual aggression, 72, 81
    impact on boys' sexual health, 34, 37

in music videos, 67
in pornography, 22, 27, 30
male insatiability, 14, 61, 121
swagger, 33
Sex, etc., 143
Sex: A Book for Teens, 140
sexting, 79–80
    prevalence, 80
    proving masculinity, 82
sexual activity
    anal sex, 41
    and alcohol, 41
    early sexual debut, 47–49
    oral sex, 40
    promiscuity, 46
    rates among teens, 40–41
    sexual intercourse, 40
sexual aggression, 4, 63–86
    against boys, 81
sexual anxiety, 30, 87, 99
sexual assault
    against boys, 83–84
    impact on boys, 83
sexual education
    Ontario, new curriculum, 62
sexual education, boys, 34–39
    effectiveness, 36–37
    from healthcare professionals, 37
    from parents, 35
    from peers, 38
    pregnancy prevention, 35, 36
    STIs, 35, 36
sexual harassment, 77–81
    definition, 77
    girls as perpetrators, 82
    impact, 78

impact on boys, 82, 124
of boys, 82–83
sexual objectification, 15–18, 18, 78
    and sexual aggression, 63, 72
    of males, 89
sexual socialization, 103
SexualityandU.ca, 143
Sexualized Media Messages and Our Children, 136
sexually explicit material. *See* pornography
sexually transmitted infections
    impact on boys, 45
    media portrayals of, 42
    rates among teens, 44–45
Shamloul, Rany, 98
Shaping Youth, 138
Shewmaker, Jennifer, 120, 121, 136, 137
Sir Mix-A-Lot, 99
Slednecks, 39, 42, 90
small penis syndrome. *See* penis size
Smith, Marshall, 19, 28, 30, 101, 112, 113, 117
Smolak, Linda, 92
Snapchat, 80
Snoop Dogg, 3
sports, 135
STDs. *See* sexually transmitted infections
Stein, Jonathan A., 92
steroids, 133
STIs. *See* sexually transmitted infections
subordination, 15

Super Mario, 11
superheroes, 90, 127
   and body image, 90
Supernatural, 58, 59, 84
T.I., 68, 99
Talk Dirty, 3
Taylor, Laramie, 66
Teen Health Source, 144
Teenage Mutant Ninja Turtles, 65
The "What's Happening to My Body?" Book for Boys, 130, 138
The Adonis Complex, 127
The Body Image Survival Guide for Parents, 126, 133
The Good Old Naughty Days, 21
The Hunger Games, 126
The Mindy Project, 59
The Real World, 39, 42, 57
The Romance of Lust, 96

Thicke, Robin, 67, 99
Thompson, Michael, 135
Tiggeman, Marika, 4, 88, 94
Transformers: Age of Extinction, 65
Trey Songz, 125
Valkenburg, Patti, 28, 29, 117
Vevo, 68
Wang, Alexander, 16
Wardy, Melissa Atkins, 109, 130
Warhaft-Nadler, Marci, 126, 128, 133
Westwood, Michael, 100, 119, 129
White Ribbon Campaign, 124
Wiggle, 3, 108
Wiseman, Rosalind, 135
YouTube, 68
Zilbergeld, Bernard, 96

NOTES

Introduction

[1] Derulo, Jason. "Wiggle" *YouTube* May 21, 2014. https://www.youtube.com/watch?v=hiP14ED28CA Accessed February 20, 2015.

[2] *Billboard* Chart History: Jason Derulo http://www.billboard.com/artist/304245/jason-derulo/chart Accessed March 2, 2015.

[3] Zhang, Yuanyuan et al. "The Relationship Between Exposure to Sexual Music Videos and Young Adults' Sexual Attitudes" *Journal of Broadcasting & Electronic Media* 52, no. 3 (2008), p. 369.

[4] Slater, Amy and Marika Tiggemann. "Body Image and Distorted Eating in Adolescent Girls and Boys: A Test of Objectification Theory." *Sex Roles* 63, no. 1-2 (2010) p. 42.

[5] Timmons, Heather. "Woman Dies After Gang Rape That Galvanized India" *New York Times* December 28, 2012 http://www.nytimes.com/2012/12/29/world/asia/condition-worsens-for-victim-of-gang-rape-in-india.html?_r=0 Accessed March 6, 2014.

[6] Schiller, Bill. "Steubenville Big Red football players stand trial on sex charges" *Toronto Star* March 9, 2013. http://www.thestar.com/news/world/2013/03/09/steubenville_big_red_football_players_stand_trial_on_sex_charges.html Accessed March 9, 2013.

[7] CBC News. "Rape, bullying led to N.S. teen's death, says mom" CBC News Online. April 9, 2013. http://www.cbc.ca/news/canada/nova-scotia/story/2013/04/09/ns-rehtaeh-parsons-suicide-rape.html Accessed April 9, 2013.

[8] Mendoza, Martha. "Girl, 15, hangs herself after photos of alleged sexual assault posted online; 3 U.S. teens charged" *Toronto Star* April 12, 2013. http://www.thestar.com/news/world/2013/04/12/girl_15_hangs_herself_after_photos_of_alleged_sexual_assault_posted_online_3_us_teens_charged.html Accessed April 12, 2013.

[9] Hill, Catherine and Holly Kearl. *Crossing the Line: Sexual Harassment at School*. Washington: AAUW, 2011, p. 11-12.

[10] Myers, D.G. *Social Psychology*. 11th ed. New York: McGraw-Hill, 2012, p. 11.

[11] Lyons, James. "'We need a sex education revolution': Parents powerless

over sexualisation of children, MP Diane Abbott claims." *The Mirror*, January 22, 2013. http://www.mirror.co.uk/news/uk-news/parents-powerless-over-sexualisation-of-children-1548660 Accessed February 16, 2013.

Chapter One

[1] Attwood, Feona. "Sexed Up: Theorizing the Sexualization of Culture" *Sexualities* 9, no. 1 (2006), p. 82.

[2] Milestone, Katie and Anneke Meyer. *Gender & Popular Culture*. Cambridge, UK: Polity Press, 2012, p. 19-21.

[3] Wang, Wendy et al. "Breadwinner Moms" *Pew Research Social & Demographic Trends* May 29, 2013 http://www.pewsocialtrends.org/2013/05/29/breadwinner-moms/ Accessed July 22, 2013.

[4] Milligan, Kevin. "What the data shows about female breadwinners in Canada" *Macleans* June 10, 2013 http://www2.macleans.ca/2013/06/10/what-the-data-shows-about-female-breadwinners-in-canada/ Accessed July 22, 2013.

[5] Huesmann, L. Rowell. "An Information Processing Model for the Development of Aggression" *Aggressive Behavior* 4, no. 1 (1988): p. 13-24.

[6] Wiederman, Michael. "The Gendered Nature of Sexual Scripts" *The Family Journal* 13, no. 4 (2005): p. 496-499.

[7] Tolman, Deborah et al. "Rethinking the Associations between Television Viewing and Adolescent Sexuality Development: Bringing Gender into Focus" *Journal of Adolescent Health* 40, no. 1 (2007): p. 84.e9-84.e10.

[8] *Don Jon*. Directed by Joseph Gordon-Levitt. Los Angeles: Voltage Pictures, 2013.

[9] Valenti, Jessica. *The Purity Myth: How America's Obsession with Virginity is Hurting Young Women*. Berkeley: Seal Press, 2009.

[10] Kim, Janna et al. "From Sex to Sexuality: Exposing the Heterosexual Script on Primetime Network Television" *Journal of Sex Research* 44, no. 2 (2007): p. 146-7, 156.

[11] Tolman et al, p. 84.e10.

[12] Fredrickson, Barbara L. and Tomi-Ann Roberts. "Objectification Theory: Toward Understanding Women's Lived Experiences and Mental Health Risks" *Psychology of Women Quarterly* 21, no.2 (1997), p. 174.

[13] American Psychological Association, Task Force on the Sexualization of

Girls. (2010).*Report of the APA Task Force on the Sexualization of Girls.* http://www.apa.org/pi/women/programs/girls/report-full.pdf, p. 1.

[14] Papadaki, Evangelia (Lina), "Feminist Perspectives on Objectification", *The Stanford Encyclopedia of Philosophy (Winter 2012 Edition)*, Edward N. Zalta (ed.), http://plato.stanford.edu/archives/win2012/entries/feminism-objectification/ Accessed February 23, 2013.

[15] Thomson Reuters. "American Apparel Files for Bankruptcy Protection" October 5, 2015. http://www.cbc.ca/news/business/american-apparel-chapter-11-bankruptcy-1.3256563 Accessed October 12, 2015.

[16] Bain, Marc. "American Apparel is in a hole , so it's good that its new CEO is not at all like Dov Charney." Quartz, June 17, 2015. http://qz.com/425294/american-apparel-is-in-a-hole-so-its-good-that-its-new-ceo-is-not-at-all-like-dov-charney/ Accessed December 7, 2015.

[17] American Apparel. "The Stretch Floral Lace Panty" *Photo Archive.* December 26, 2013. http://www.americanapparel.net/photovideo/photo/details/index.html?i=3116&n=8 Accessed January 22, 2014.

[18] Sanghani. Radhika. "Why these naked women make me feel uncomfortable." *The Telegraph* December 4, 2014 http://www.telegraph.co.uk/women/womens-life/11273072/Naked-celebrity-women-make-me-feel-uncomfortable.html Accessed December 4, 2014.

[19] Vagianos, Alanna. "Sexist Ad Campaign Reminds Women They're Nothing More than Objects." *The Huffington Post.* December 4, 2015. http://www.huffingtonpost.com/entry/sexist-i-love-ugly-ad-campaign-reminds-women-they-are-objects_5661a889e4b072e9d1c5bbf5?cps=gravity_2246_-7225116397627993971 Accessed December 4, 2015.

[20] Hooters. "Jon Gruden and a bunch of Hooters Girls walk into a stadium…" *YouTube* August 27, 2014. https://www.youtube.com/watch?v=kqsMbESWdR8 Accessed December 7, 2015.

[21] Owens, Eric W. et al. "The Impact of Internet Pornography on Adolescents: A Review of the Research" *Sexual Addiction and Compulsivity* 19, no 1-2 (2012), p. 106.

Chapter Two

[1] Carroll, Jason S. "Generation XXX: Pornography Acceptance and Use Among Emerging Adults." *Journal of Adolescent Research* 23, no. 1 (2008), p. 23.

[2] Smith, Marshall. "Youth Viewing Sexually Explicit Material Online: Addressing the Elephant on the Screen" *Sexuality Research and Social Policy.* 10, no.1 (2013): p. 65.

[3] Both titles were shown on www.xnxx.com when I accessed the site on February 6, 2014. The Wonder Woman film was animated and designed to look like an episode of *Justice League.*

[4] Dopp, Hans-Jurgen et al. *1000 Erotic Works of Genius.* New York: Parkstone Press, 2008, p. 11.

[5] Editors of Encyclopaedia Britannica. "Phallicism" *Encyclopaedia Britannica.* http://www.britannica.com/EBchecked/topic/455022/phallicism Accessed August 1, 2013.

[6] Holland, Jack. *Misogyny: The World's Oldest Prejudice.* New York: Carroll & Graf, 2006, p. 12-35.

[7] Eroti Cart. "I Modi" *The History of Erotic Art.* http://www.eroti-cart.com/i-modi-c-93 Accessed January 13, 2014.

[8] Néret, Gilles. *Erotica Universalis.* Koln: Taschen, 1994. Electronic Edition.

[9] Toulalan, Sarah. *Imagining Sex: Pornography and Bodies in Seventeenth-Century England.* Oxford: Oxford University Press, 2007. Kindle Edition.

[10] Cleland, John. *Memoirs of Fanny Hill: A New and Genuine Edition from the Original Text.* Paris: Isidore Liseux. Reprinted by Amazon Digital Services. (The Kindle edition includes no page numbers.)

[11] Sade, Marquis de. *Juliette.* Translated by Austryn Wainhouse. New York: Grove House, 1968.

[12] Jenkins, John Philip. "Obscenity" *Encyclopaedia Britannica* http://www.britannica.com/EBchecked/topic/424001/obscenity Accessed July 29, 2013.

[13] *The Erotica Bibliophile.* http://www.eroticabibliophile.com/illustrations_index.php. Accessed January 13, 2014.

[14] My Porno Project. "The Good Old Naughty Days (by all means)" *mypornoproject.com.* May 24, 2012. http://mypornoproject.com/2012/05/24/the-good-old-naughty-days-by-all-means/ Accessed January 14, 2014. The link has since been taken down but the film can be seen at http://www.xvideos.com/video7522081/the_good_old_naughty_days as of July, 2015.

[15] Weber, Mathias et al. "Peers, Parents and Pornography: Exploring Adolescents' Exposure to Sexually Explicit Material and Its Developmental Correlates" *Sexuality & Culture* 16, no. 4 (2012), p. 409-10.

[16] Toulalan, Sarah.

[17] Owens, Eric et al. "The Impact of Internet Pornography on Adolescents: A Review of the Research" *Sexual Addiction and Compulsivity* 19, no 1-2, (2012), p. 100.

[18] GFI Software. *2011 Parent-Teen Internet Safety Report.* June 2011. http://www.gfi.com/documents/GFI%20_2011_parent_teen_internet_safety_report_june.pdf Accessed April 27, 2013.

[19] Sexperience/Channel 4. *Teen Sex Survey.* http://sexperienceuk.channel4.com/teen-sex-survey. Accessed April 27, 2013.

[20] Sabina, Chiara et al. "The Nature and Dynamics of Internet Pornography Exposure for Youth." *CyberPsychology & Behavior* 11, no. 6 (2008), p. 692.

[21] Brown, Jane D. and Kelly L'Engle. "X-Rated: Sexual Attitudes and Behaviors Associated with U.S. Early Adolescents' Exposure to Sexually Explicit Media." *Communication Research* 36, no. 1, (2009), p. 139.

[22] Wright, Paul J. et al. "Research on Sex in the Media: What Do We Know About Effects on Children and Adolescents" in *Handbook of Children and the Media.* 2nd ed. Dorothy G. Singer and Jerome L. Singer, eds, Los Angeles: Sage Publications, 2012. p. 292.

[23] BBC News Online. "Kids' top searches include 'porn'". August 12, 2009. http://news.bbc.co.uk/2/hi/technology/8197143.stm Accessed April 27, 2013.

[24] It was hard to gauge the exact number of sexually active teens among the overall male adolescent population, but estimates from various studies show that one-third of adolescent males are sexually active. Population statistics for 2007 indicate that there are 3.5 million males aged 10-19 in the UK meaning just over one million (one-third) are sexually active. If 5% of those boys are daily porn users, that could mean upwards of 50,000 boys watching porn on a regular basis, a not insignificant number.

[25] Flood, Michael. "The Harms of Pornography Exposure Among Children and Young People." *Child Abuse Review* 18, no. 6 (2009), p. 386.

[26] Weber et al, p. 411, 416.

[27] Löfgren-Mårtenson, Lotta and Sven-Axel Månsson. "Lust, Love, and Life: A Qualitative Study of Swedish Adolescents' Perceptions and Experiences with Pornography" *Journal of Sex Research.* 47, no. 6 (2010): p. 1-12.

[28] Brown, Jane D. and Kelly L'Engle. "X-Rated: Sexual Attitudes and Behaviors Associated with U.S. Early Adolescents' Exposure to Sexually Explicit Media." *Communication Research* 36, no. 1, (2009), p. 139.

[29] Braun-Courville, D.K. and Mary Rojas. "Exposure to Sexually Explicit Web Sites and Adolescent Sexual Attitudes and Behaviours." *Journal of Adolescent Health* 45, no.2 (2009), 161.
[30] Owens, Eric W. et al, p. 100.
[31] Dines, Gail. *Pornland: How Porn Has Hijacked Our Sexuality*. Boston: Beacon Press, 2010, p. 13-14.
[32] Benwell, Max. "Why you should be worried about Playboy dropping naked women from its pages." *Independent* October 20, 2015. http://www.independent.co.uk/voices/why-you-should-be-worried-about-playboy-dropping-naked-women-from-its-pages-a6692756.html Accessed November 24, 2015.
[33] Playboy. "Coed Girls" *Playboy Plus* http://www.playboyplus.com/category/coed-girls/ Accessed December 8, 2015.
[34] Playboy. "Special Editions" *Playboy Plus* http://www.playboyplus.com/category/special-editions/ Accessed December 8, 2015.
[35] Xnxx. http://www.xnxx.com/ Accessed March 25, 2013.
[36] Foubert, John D. "Pornography Viewing among Fraternity Men: Effects on Bystander Intervention, Rape Myth Acceptance and Behavioral Intent to Commit Sexual Assault" *Sexual Addiction and Compulsivity*. 18, no. 4 (2011), p. 213.
[37] Dines, p. 17-20.
[38] Attwood, Feona. "'Tits and ass and porn and fighting': Male heterosexuality in magazines for men" *International Journal of Cultural Studies* 8, no. 1 (2005), p. 91.
[39] Löfgren-Mårtenson, Lotta and Sven-Axel Månsson, p. 6-10.
[40] Smith, p. 71.
[41] Weber at al, p. 419.
[42] Peter, Jochen and Patti M. Valkenburg. "Processes Underlying the Effects of Adolescents' Use of Sexually Explicit Internet Material: The Role of Perceived Realism" *Communication Research* 37, no. 3: 2010, p. 377.
[43] Peter, Jochen and Patti M. Valkenburg. "Adolescents' Exposure to Sexually Explicit Internet Material and Sexual Preoccupancy: A Three-Wave Panel Study." *Media Psychology* 11, no. 2 : 2008, p. 226-227.
[44] Peter and Valkenburg, 2010, *Communication Research*. p. 377.
[45] Carroll Jason S., p. 6-30.
[46] Peter and Valkenburg, 2010, 377.
[47] Smith, p. 73.
[48] Flood, p. 394-5.

Chapter Three

[1] Warner Bros. Television et al. "Pilot" *Arrow*. October 10, 2012
[2] Giese, Rachel. "The Talk: A new sex ed for boys" *The Walrus* April 2014, p. 29.
[3] Ott, Mary A. "Examining the Development and Sexual Behavior of Adolescent Males" *Journal of Adolescent Health* 46, no. 4, Supplement (2010), S3-S11.
[4] World Health Organization. "Defining sexual health" http://www.who.int/reproductivehealth/topics/sexual_health/sh_definitions/en/index.html Accessed September 16, 2013.
[5] Giese, p. 28.
[6] Donaldson, Abigail et al. "Receipt of Sexual Health Information From Parents, Teachers, and Healthcare Providers by Sexually Experienced US Adolescents" *Journal of Adolescent Health* 53, no. 2 (2013): p. 235-240.
[7] National Campaign to Prevent Teen Pregnancy. "Parent-Child Communication About Sex and Related Topics" *Science Says* no. 25 (May 2006): p. 3.
[8] Donaldson.
[9] Guttmacher Institute, "Facts on American Teens' Sources of Information About Sex" *In Brief* February, 2012

http://www.guttmacher.org/pubs/FB-Teen-Sex-Ed.html Accessed June 17, 2013.

[10] Giese, p. 28-29.
[11] Ayala, Jessica et al. *Promoting Sexual Health for Young Men.* Calgary: Calgary Sexual Health Centre, 2008, p. 8, 28.
[12] Several studies have produced similar results, including: Lindberg, Laura Duberstein. "Consequences of Sex Education on Teen and Young Adult Sexual Behaviors and Outcomes" *Journal of Adolescent Health* 51, no. 4 (2012), p. 332-338 and Kirby, Douglas B. "The Impact of Abstinence and Comprehensive Sex and STD/HIV Education Programs on Adolescent Sexual Behaviour" *Sexuality Research and Social Policy*. 5, no. 3 (2008), p. 18-27.
[13] Taylor, Laramie D. "All for Him: Articles About Sex in American Lad Magazines" *Sex Roles* 52, no. 3-4, (2005), p. 154.
[14] The Guttmacher report provides some interesting numbers on abstinence: 28% of male and 23% of female teens received abstinence education but no birth control information in the years between 2006 and 2008, an increase from 8-9% from 1995, indicating that abstinence education is increasing, at least in the United States.

[15] Ayala, p. 4-5.
[16] Marcell, Arik A. et al. "Male Adolescent Sexual and Reproductive Health Care" *Pediatrics* 128, no. 6 (2011): p. 1658.
[17] Marsiglio,W., Ries, A., Sonenstein, F., Troccoli, K. & Whitehead,W. *It's a GuyThing: Boys, Young Men, and Teen Pregnancy Prevention*. Washington, DC: National Campaign to Prevent Teen, 2006, p. 5.

[18] National Campaign to End Teen Pregnancy. "Adolescent Boys' Use of Health Services" *Science Says* no. 25 (July 2006): p. 1-4.
[19] National Campaign to End Teen Pregnancy. "Adolescent Girls' Use of Health Services" *Science Says* no. 25 (September 2006): p. 1-4.
[20] Sabina, Chiara et al. "The Nature and Dynamics of Internet Pornography Exposure for Youth." *CyberPsychology & Behavior* 11, no. 6 (2008), p. 692.
[21] Ayala, p. 27-28.
[22] Hampton, Mary Rucklos et al."Influence of Teens' Perceptions of Parental Disapproval and Peer Behaviour on Their Initiation of Sexual Intercourse" *The Canadian Journal of Human Sexuality*. 14, no. 3-4 (2005): p, 105.
[23] Ayala, p. 29.
[24] Humphreys. Terry. "Understanding Sexual Consent: An Empirical Investigation of the Normative Script for Young Heterosexual Adults" in *Making Sense of Sexual Consent* Mark Cowling, Paul Reynolds, eds., Surrey, UK: Ashgate, 2004, p. 213.
[25] Claxton, Shannon E. and Manfred H. M. van Dulmen. "Casual Sexual Relationships and Experiences in Emerging Adulthood" *Emerging Adulthood* 1, no. 2 (2013), p. 138-150.
[26] Rosin, Hanna. "Boys on the Side" *The Atlantic* September 2012 http://www.theatlantic.com/magazine/archive/2012/09/boys-on-the-side/309062/ Accessed December 21, 2014.
[27] Eyal, Keren and Keli Finnerty. "The Portrayal of Sexual Intercourse on Television: How, Who, and With What Consequences?" *Mass Communication and Society*. 12, no. 2, (2009) p. 157, 162.
[28] Gunasekera, Hasantha et al. "Sex and drugs in popular movies: an analysis of the top 200 films." *Journal of the Royal Society of Medicine* 98, no. 10 (2005), p. 464-466.
[29] Centers for Disease Control. *Youth Online: High School YRBS: United States 1991-2013 Results* http://nccd.cdc.gov/youthonline/App/Results.aspx?TT=A&OUT=0&SID=HS&QID=QQ&LID=XX&YID=YY&LID2=&YID2=&COL=S&ROW1=N&ROW2=N&HT=C4&LCT=LL&FS=S1&FR=R1&FG=G1&FSL=S1&FRL=R1&FGL=G1&PV=&TST=&C1=&C2=&QP=G&DP=1&VA=CI&CS=Y&SYID=&EYID=&SC=DEFAULT&SO=ASC

Accessed January 6, 2015.
[30] SIECCAN. "Statistics Related to Trends in the Sexual Behaviours of Canadian Teenagers" *Check the Research* July/August 2012, http://sexualityandu.ca/uploads/files/CTR_TeenageStatistics_JULYAUG2012-EN.pdf Accessed November 15, 2012.
[31] SIECCAN, 2012.

[32] Mosher, William D. et al. "Sexual Behavior and Selected Health Measures: Men and Women 15-44 Years of Age, United States 2002" *Advance Data From Vital and Health Statistics* No. 362 (2005) Atlanta: Centers for Disease Control. p. 21
[33] Copen, Casey et al. "Prevalence and Timing of Oral Sex with Opposite-sex Partners Among Females and Males Aged 15-24 Years: United States, 2007-2010. *National Health Statistics Reports* No. 56 (2012) Atlanta: Centers for Disease Control. p. 10.
[34] Claxton and van Dulmen, p. 138-150.
[35] Heldman, Caroline and Lisa Wade. "Hook-Up Culture: Setting a New Research Agenda" *Sexuality Research and Social Policy*. 7, no. 4 (2010), p. 328.
[36] Eyal and Finnerty, p. 163.
[37] Stern, Susannah and Jane D. Brown. "From Twin Beds to Sex at Your Fingertips: Teen Sexuality in Movies, Music, Television, and the Internet, 1950 to 2005 in *Changing Portrayal of Adolescents in Media Since 1950*. London: Oxford University Press (2008), p. 321.
[38] Farrar, Kirstie M. "Sexual Intercourse on Television: Do Safe Sex Messages Matter?" *Journal of Broadcasting & Electronic Media* 50, no. 4 (2006), p. 637.
[39] Kunkel, Dale et al. *Sex on TV 4*. Menlo Park: Kaiser Family Foundation (2005), p. 35, 51-55.
[40] Collins, RL et al. "Entertainment television as healthy sex educator: the impact of condom-efficacy information in an episode of Friends" *Pediatrics* 112, no. 5 (2003), p. 1115-21.
[41] Farrar, Kirstie M., p. 645.
[42] Smith, Marshall. "Youth Viewing Sexually Explicit Material Online: Addressing the Elephant on the Screen." *Sexuality Reseearch and Social Policy*. 10, no. 1 (2013), p. 62.
[43] Halpern-Felsher, Bonnie et al. "Oral Versus Vaginal Sex Among Adolescents: Perceptions, Attitudes, and Behavior." *Pediatrics* 115, no. 4 (2005): p. 845-851.
[44] LeWine, Howard. "HPV transmission during oral sex a growing cause of mouth and throat cancer." *Harvard Health Blog* June 4, 2013. http://www.health.harvard.edu/blog/hpv-transmission-during-oral-sex-a-growing-cause-of-mouth-and-throat-cancer-201306046346 Accessed

October 16, 2013.
[45] Centers for Disease Control and Prevention. *Genital HPV Infection—Fact Sheet* July 25, 2013. http://www.cdc.gov/std/hpv/stdfact-hpv.htm Accessed October 16, 2013.
[46] Guttmacher Institute. "Facts on American Teens' Sexual and Reproductive Health." *In Brief* February 2012, p. 2.
[47] The Society of Obstetricians and Gynaecologists of Canada. "Health Complications and Risks of HPV" *HPV Info* website http://www.hpvinfo.ca/teens/health-complications-and-risks-of-hpv/ Accessed April 7, 2013.
[48] National Advisory Committee on Immunization. "Statement on Human Papillomavirus Vaccine" *Canada Communicable Disease Report* 33, ACS-2 (2007), p. 1-7.
[49] Centers for Disease Control and Prevention. *2011 Sexually Transmitted Diseases Surveillance: Chlamydia.* http://www.cdc.gov/std/stats11/tables/10.htm Accessed April 7, 2013.
[50] Public Health Agency of Canada. *Reported cases and rates of Chlamydia by age group and sex, 1991 to 2009* http://www.phac-aspc.gc.ca/std-mts/sti-its_tab/chlamydia-eng.php Accessed April 7, 2013.
[51] Public Health Agency of Canada. *Reported cases and rates of infectious syphilis by age group and sex, 1993 to 2009* http://www.phac-aspc.gc.ca/std-mts/sti-its_tab/syphilis-eng.php Accessed April 7, 2013.
[52] Centers for Disease Control and Prevention. *2011 Sexually Transmitted Diseases Surveillance: Primary and Secondary Syphilis.* http://www.cdc.gov/std/stats11/tables/34.htm Accessed April 7, 2013.
[53] Guttmacher Institute. "Facts on American Teens' Sexual and Reproductive Health" *In Brief* February 2012, p. 2.
[54] Centers for Disease Control and Prevention. *HIV Surveillance Report*, no. 22 (2010), p. 6.
[55] Public Health Agency of Canada. *At A Glance—HIV and AIDS in Canada: Surveillance Report to December 31st, 2011.* http://www.phac-aspc.gc.ca/aids-sida/publication/survreport/2011/dec/index-eng.php Accessed April 7, 2013.
[56] Centers for Disease Control and Prevention. *2011 Sexually Transmitted Diseases Surveillance: Gonorrhea.* http://www.cdc.gov/std/stats11/tables/21.htm Accessed April 7, 2013.
[57] Public Health Agency of Canada. *Reported cases and rates of gonorrhea by age group and sex, 1980 to 2009* http://www.phac-aspc.gc.ca/std-mts/sti-its_tab/gonorrhea-eng.php Accessed April 7, 2013.
[58] Marcell, e1662.
[59] Epididymitis is an inflammation of the tube that carries sperm. It can become a chronic problem if left untreated. Mayo Clinic. Epididymitis.

http://www.mayoclinic.com/health/epididymitis/DS00603 Accessed October 15, 2013.
[60] Centers for Disease Control and Prevention. "Sexual Risk Behavior: HIV, STD, & Teen Pregnancy Prevention" August 26, 2013.
http://www.cdc.gov/healthyyouth/sexualbehaviors/index.htm Accessed September 10, 2013.
[61] Heldman, Caroline and Lisa Wade. "Hook-Up Culture: Setting a New Research Agenda" *Sexuality Research and Social Policy*. 7, no. 4 (2010), p. 326.
[62] Centers for Disease Control. *Youth Online: High School YRBS: United States 1991-2013 Results*
http://nccd.cdc.gov/youthonline/App/Results.aspx?TT=A&OUT=0&SID=HS&QID=QQ&LID=XX&YID=YY&LID2=&YID2=&COL=S&ROW1=N&ROW2=N&HT=C4&LCT=LL&FS=S1&FR=R1&FG=G1&FSL=S1&FRL=R1&FGL=G1&PV=&TST=&C1=&C2=&QP=G&DP=1&VA=CI&CS=Y&SYID=&EYID=&SC=DEFAULT&SO=ASC
Accessed January 6, 2015.
[63] Guttmacher, "Facts on Young Men's Sexual and Reproductive Health".
[64] Boyce, William et al. "Sexual Health of Canadian Youth: Findings from the *Canadian Youth, Sexual Health, and HIV/AIDS Study*" *Canadian Journal of Human Sexuality*, 15, no. 2 (2006), p. 62.
[65] Marcell, p. e1664.
[66] Ayala et al, p. 10.
[67] Luder, Marie-Thérèse et al. "Associations Between Online Pornography and Sexual Behavior Among Adolescents: Myth or Reality?" *Archives of Sexual Behavior* 40, no. 5 (2011), p. 1033.
[68] Centers for Disease Control and Prevention. "Teen Pregnancy Prevention and United States Students" 2013.
http://www.cdc.gov/healthyyouth/yrbs/pdf/us_pregnancy_combo.pdf Accessed December 21, 2014.
[69] Bielski, Zosia. "Why teen pregnancy is on the rise again in Canada (and spiking in these provinces) *The Globe and Mail* January 29, 2013.
http://www.theglobeandmail.com/life/health-and-fitness/health/why-teen-pregnancy-is-on-the-rise-again-in-canada-and-spiking-in-these-provinces/article7927983/ Accessed Jun3 15, 2013.
[70] Office for National Statistics. "Conceptions in England and Wales, 2012" *Statistical Bulletin* February, 2014.
http://www.ons.gov.uk/ons/rel/vsob1/conception-statistics--england-and-wales/2012/2012-conceptions-statistical-bulletin.html Accessed January 7, 2015.
[71] National Campaign to Prevent Teen and Unplanned Pregnancy. *Fast Facts: Teen Pregnancy in the United States* August 2014.
http://thenationalcampaign.org/sites/default/files/resource-primary-

download/fast_facts_-_teen_pregnancy_in_the_united_states_aug_2014_0.pdf Accessed December 21, 2014.

[72] Caminis, Argyro et al. "Psychosocial predictors or sexual initiation and high-risk sexual behaviors in early adolescence" *Child and Adolescent Psychiatry and Mental Health* 1, no. 14. (2007) http://www.capmh.com/content/1/1/14 Accessed November 12, 2012.

[73] Kaestle, Christine et al. "Young Age at First Sexual Intercourse and Sexually Transmitted Infections in Adolescents and Young Adults" *American Journal of Epidemiology* 161, no. 8 (2005): p. 774.

[74] Price, Myeshia N. And Janet Shibley Hyde. "When Two Isn't Better Than One: Predictors of Early Sexual Activity in Adolescence Using a Cumulative Risk Model" *Journal of Youth and Adolescence* 38, no. 8 (2009) p, 1067-1069.

[75] Udell, Wadiya et al. "The Relationship Between Early Sexual Debut and Psychosocial Outcomes: A Longitudinal Study of Dutch Adolescents" *Archives of Sexual Behavior* 39, no. 5 (2010), p. 1141.

[76] Caminis, Argyro et al.

[77] Price and Hyde, p. 1067-1069.

[78] Levant, Ronald F. "Men and Masculinity," in Vol. 2 of *Encyclopedia of Women and Gender: Sex Similarities and Differences and the Impact of Society on Gender.* ed. Judith Worrell. (San Diego: Academic Press, 2001), 717-727. Levant has written extensively on family and gender psychology. His full bio is available at http://www.drronaldlevant.com/bio.html.

[79] Giordano, Peggy et al. "Gender and the Meanings of Adolescent Romantic Relationships: A Focus on Boys" *American Sociological Review* 71, no. 2 (2006), p. 261.

[80] Ott, p. S8.

[81] Boyce, p. 63.

[82] Giordano, Peggy et al., p. 283.

[83] Giese, p. 32.

Chapter Four

[1] Coy, Maddy et al. *'Sex without consent, I suppose that is rape':* How young people in

England understand sexual consent. London: Office of the Children's Commissioner, 2013.

[2] Williams, Sally. "Campus nightmare: female students on the rise of sexual harassment *The Guardian* October 11, 2014 http://www.theguardian.com/education/2014/oct/11/campus-nightmare-female-students-rise-sexual-harassment Accessed October 13, 2014.

[3] Humphreys. Terry. "Understanding Sexual Consent: An Empirical Investigation of the Normative Script for Young Heterosexual Adults" in *Making Sense of Sexual Consent* Mark Cowling, Paul Reynolds, eds., Surrey, UK: Ashgate, 2004, p. 223.

[4] Coy et al.

[5] Jozkowski, Kristen N. et al. "Consenting to Sexual Activity: The Development and Psychometric Assessment of Dual Measures of Consent" *Archives of Sexual Behaviour* 43, no. 3 (2014), p. 438.

[6] Humphreys, Terry and Ed Herold. "Sexual Consent in Heterosexual Relationships: Development of a New Measure" *Sex Roles* 57, no. 3 (2007), p. 313.

[7] Coy et al, p. 11.

[8] Humphreys and Herold, 2007, p. 314.

[9] Donnelly, Matthew Scott. "Are You The One Aftermath: Jessica Says Her Hookup With Anthony Lasted 30 Seconds" *MTV* October 10, 2014 http://www.mtv.com/news/1957535/are-you-the-one-anthony-jessica-pound-town/ Accessed October 21, 2014.

[10] Krassas, Nicole et al. "'Master Your Johnson': Sexual Rhetoric in *Maxim* and *Stuff* Magazines" *Sexuality & Culture* 7, no. 3. (2003), p. 114.

[11] FHM. "FHM's best ever Ladies' confessions: the top 100" *FHM*.com http://www.fhm.com/girls/true-confessions April, 2009. Accessed November 29, 2012. Although first published in 2009, this article was being promoted on the FHM website when I visited it in late 2012.

[12] Hampton, Mary R.et al. "Influence of Teens' Perceptions of Parental Disapproval and Peer Behaviour on Their Initiation of Sexual Intercourse" *The Canadian Journal of Human Sexuality*, 14, no. 3-4 (2005): 114-115.

[13] Giese, Rachel. "The Talk: A new sex ed for boys *The Walrus* April 2014, p. 29.

[14] Coy et al. p. 43-44.

[15] Gilroy, Kay. "Stop including sexual violence on 'Supernatural'" *Change.org* http://www.change.org/p/the-cw-television-network-stop-including-sexual-violence-on-supernatural Accessed October 19, 2014

[16] Warner Bros. Television. "Caged Heat" *Supernatural* December 3, 2010.

[17] Warner Bros. Television. "Devil May Care" *Supernatural* October 15, 2013.

[18] Warner Bros. Television. "Rock and a Hard Place" *Supernatural* November 26, 2013.
[19] Universal Television. "I Slipped" *The Mindy Project.* October 7, 2014.
[20] Humphreys, 2004, p. 209.
[21] Humphreys and Herold, 2007, p. 313.
[22] Giese, p. 29.
[23] White House. *1 is 2 Many.* YouTube https://www.youtube.com/watch?v=xLdElcv5qqc Accessed October 13, 2014.
[24] It's On Us. *It's On Us.* https://www.youtube.com/watch?v=wNMZo31LziM#t=11 Accessed October 13, 2014.
[25] Associated Press. "California adopts 'yes means yes' law aiming to curb campus sexual assaults." *Globe and Mail.* September 29, 2014. http://www.theglobeandmail.com/news/world/california-adopts-yes-means-yes-law-aiming-to-curb-campus-sex-assaults/article20823487/ Accessed October 13, 2014.
[26] Kaminer, Ariel. "Cuomo Orders SUNY to Overhaul Its Sexual Assault Rules" *New York Times* http://www.nytimes.com/2014/10/03/nyregion/cuomo-orders-suny-to-overhaul-its-sexual-assault-rules.html Accessed October 13, 2014.
[27] Leslie, Keith. "Ontario's new sex ed curriculum will teach consent in grade 2" *Global News.* February 23, 2015. http://globalnews.ca/news/1844927/ontario-revises-sex-education-curriculum/ Accessed December 8, 2015.
[28] Snowdon, Wallis. "Alberta school boards want consent added to sex-education curriculum" *CBC News.* November 18, 2015. http://www.cbc.ca/news/canada/edmonton/alberta-school-boards-want-consent-added-to-sex-education-curriculum-1.3324110 Accessed December 8, 2015.
[29] B.C. Almanac. "B.C. sex-ed curriculum should follow Ontario's lead: expert" *CBC News.* March 3, 2015. http://www.cbc.ca/news/canada/british-columbia/b-c-sex-ed-curriculum-should-follow-ontario-s-lead-expert-1.2979102 Accessed December 8, 2015.

Chapter Five

[1] Jhally, Sut. *Dreamworlds 3: Desire, Sex and Power in Music Video* Transcript. Northampton, MA: Media Education Foundation, 2007.
[2] Washington State University. "Men's magazine reading, unwanted sexual behaviors linked." *WSU News* May 27, 2014.

https://news.wsu.edu/2014/05/27/study-links-mens-magazine-readers-unwanted-sexual-behaviors/#.VVI-Co5Vikp Accessed May 12, 2015.
[3] Jhally.
[4] Nintendo. "Fire Emblem:Awakening" http://fireemblem.nintendo.com/characters/index.html Accessed March 10, 2013.
[5] Markovitz, Adam. "Where's the love? The sudden death of the Hollywood sex scene" *Entertainment Weekly* March 14, 2013.
[6] *Iron Man 3*. Directed by Shane Black. Manhattan Beach, CA: Marvel Studios, 2013.
[7] *Transformers: Age of Extinction*. Directed by Michael Bay. Los Angeles: Paramount Pictures, 2014.
[8] Common Sense Media "Teenage Mutant Ninja Turtles" *Common Sense Media* August 8, 2014 https://www.commonsensemedia.org/movie-reviews/teenage-mutant-ninja-turtles Accessed October 30, 2014.
[9] Nuts Magazine. "Assess My Breasts" *Nuts* http://www.nuts.co.uk/69084/assess-my-breasts Accessed December 9, 2012 and February 5, 2014.
[10] Zoo Magazine. "How to get the most from ZOO Real Girls: Booking shows, chatting, and more. http://www.zootoday.com/girls/real-girls/how-to-get-the-most-from-zoo-real-girls--booking-shows--chatting---more Accessed August, 2014.
[11] *Playboy* "Girls" http://www.playboy.com/girls Accessed November 24, 2015.
[12] Taylor, Laramie D. "All for Him: Articles About Sex in American Lad Magazines" *Sex Roles* 52, no. 3-4, (2005), p. 153-163.
[13] Krassas, Nicole et al. "'Master Your Johnson': Sexual Rhetoric in *Maxim* and *Stuff* Magazines" *Sexuality & Culture* 7, no. 3. (2003), p. 115.
[14] Flo Rida. "My House" *You Tube* September 24, 2015. https://www.youtube.com/watch?v=uo35R9zQsAI Accessed December 9, 2015.
[15] Fetty Wap. "679" *You Tube* May 14, 2015 https://www.youtube.com/watch?v=ELNgQFPdgrA Accessed December 8, 2015.
[16] Travis Scott. "Antidote" *YouTube* September 18, 2015. https://www.youtube.com/watch?v=KnZ8h3MRuYg Accessed December 9, 2015.
[17] Cyrus, Miley. "Wrecking Ball" *YouTube* September 9, 2013. http://www.youtube.com/watch?v=My2FRPA3Gf8 Accessed February 3, 2014.
[18] Knowles, Beyoncé. "Drunk in Love" *YouTube* December 16, 2013 http://www.youtube.com/watch?v=p1JPKLa-Ofc Accessed December

17, 2013.
[19] Gomez, Selena. "Good for You" *YouTube* August 18, 2015. https://www.youtube.com/watch?v=DXKHCgNFk1I Accessed December 9, 2015.
[20] Ryan, Kathryn. "The Relationship between Rape Myths and Sexual Scripts: The Social Construction of Rape" *Sex Roles* 65, no. 11-12 (2011), p. 779.
[21] Lil Wayne "Love Me Featuring Drake" YouTube http://www.youtube.com/watch?v=KY44zvhWhp4 February 14, 2013. Accessed March 15, 2013.
[22] A$AP Rocky. *F**kin Problems* Rapgenius website. http://rapgenius.com/Asap-rocky-fuckin-problems-lyrics Accessed March 20, 2013.
[23] 50 Cent. *Animal Ambition.* Vevo http://www.vevo.com/watch/50-cent/animal-ambition/USV6R1490005 Accessed June 25, 2014.
[24] T.I. *No Mediocre* Rapgenius website http://rapgenius.com/Ti-no-mediocre-lyrics Accessed June 25, 2014.
[25] Primack, Brian A. et al. "Exposure to Sexual Lyrics and Sexual Experience Among Urban Adolescents" *American Journal of Preventive Medicine* 36, no. 4 (2009), p. 322.
[26] Martino, Steven et al. "Exposure to Degrading Versus Nondegrading Music Lyrics and Sexual Behavior Among Youth. *Pediatrics* 118, no. 2 (2006), p. 437.
[27] Bradley, Ryan and Jessi Hempl. "YouTube to launch music streaming service, take on Spotify." CNN Money website, March 5, 2013 http://tech.fortune.cnn.com/2013/03/05/youtube-streaming/ Accessed March 17, 2013.
[28] Nielsen Holdings. "Music Discovery Still Dominated by Radio, Says Nielsen Music 360 Report." August 14, 2012. http://www.nielsen.com/us/en/press-room/2012/music-discovery-still-dominated-by-radio--says-nielsen-music-360.html Accessed March 17, 2013.
[29] Vevo. *Vevo U.S. Music Video Viewership*, August 2012. https://sparkpr.box.com/s/vmyqedphfpb6xnev0pj9 Accessed March 17, 2013.
[30] Arnett, Jeffrey Jensen. "The Sounds of Sex: Sex in Teens' Music and Music Videos" *Sexual Teens, Sexual Media: Investigating Media's Influence on Adolescent Sexuality.* Jane D. Brown et al, eds. Mahwah, NJ: Lawrence Erlbaum Associates, 2002, p. 256-7.
[31] Hustler 3D Game. http://www.hustler3dgame.com/ Accessed December 6, 2012 and again October 3, 2014.
[32] FHM. "FHM's best ever Ladies' confessions: the top 100" *FHM*.com

http://www.fhm.com/girls/true-confessions April, 2009. Accessed November 29, 2012.

[33] Earp, Jeremy. "Lessons from Steubenville: Part 2 of an Interview with Jackson Katz" *Media Education Foundation* website.
http://www.mediaed.org/blog/?p=1696 March 21, 2013. Accessed March 21, 2013.

[34] Coy, Maddy and Miranda A.H. Horvath. "'Lads' Mags', Young Men's Attitudes towards Women and Acceptance of Myths about Sexual Aggression." *Feminism & Psychology*. 20, no. 2 (2010), p. 4.

[35] Horvath, Miranda H. et al. "'Lights on at the end of the party': Are lads' mags mainstreaming dangerous sexism?" *British Journal of Psychology*. 103, no. 4 (2012): p. 454-471.

[36] The first quote is from the lad magazine, the second from a convicted rapist.

[37] Dines, p. 17-20.

[38] GonzoXXXMovies http://www.gonzoxxxmovies.com/ Accessed June 20, 2014.

[39] Peter, Jochen and Patti M. Valkenburg. "Adolescents' Exposure to Sexually Explicit Internet Material and Notions of Women as Sex Objects: Assessing Causality and Underlying Processes" *Journal of Communication* 58, no. 3: 2009, cited in Owens, Eric W. et al. "The Impact of Internet Pornography on Adolescents: A Review of the Research" *Sexual Addiction and Compulsivity* 19, no 1-2. :2012, p. 106.

[40] Dill, Karen E. et al. "Effects of exposure to sex-stereotyped video game characters on tolerance of sexual harassment." *Journal of Experimental Social Psychology* 44, no.5 (2008), p. 1402-1408.

[41] Hust, Stacy et al. "Establishing and adhering to sexual consent: The association of reading magazines and college students' sexual consent negotiation." *Journal of Sex Research* 51, no. 3 (2014), p. 280-290.

[42] Galdi, Silvia et al. "Objectifying Media: Their Effect on Gender Role Norms and Sexual Harassment of Women." *Psychology of Women Quarterly* 38, no. 3 (2014), p. 13.

[43] Littleton, Heather et al. "Priming of Consensual and Nonconsensual Sexual Scripts: An Experimental Test of the Role of Scripts in Rape Attributions" *Sex Roles* 54, no. 7-8 (2006), p. 557.

[44] Maxwell, Christopher D. et al. "The Nature and Predictors of Sexual Victimization and Offending Among Adolescents" *Journal of Youth and Adolescence* 32, no. 6 (2003), p. 472.

[45] Baker, Katie J.M. "Anonymous Leaks Horrifying Video of Steubenville High Schoolers Joking About Raping a Teenager 'Deader Than Trayvon Martin'" Jezebel January 2, 2103.

http://jezebel.com/5972553/anonymous-leaks-horrifying-video-of-steubenville-high-schoolers-joking-about-raping-a-teenager-deader-than-trayvon-martin Accessed March 18, 2013.

[46] Carmon, Irin. "Four lessons from Steubenville" *Salon* March 18, 2013. http://www.salon.com/2013/03/18/four_lessons_from_steubenville/ Accessed March 18, 2013.

[47] Littleton, Heather. "Rape Myths and Beyond: A Commentary on Edwards and Colleagues (2011)" *Sex Roles* 65, no. 11-12 (2011), p. 794.

[48] Maxwell, Christopher D. et al. "The Nature and Predictors of Sexual Victimization and Offending Among Adolescents" *Journal of Youth and Adolescence* 32, no. 6 (2003), p. 467.

[49] Littleton, 2011, p. 794.

[50] McMahon, Sarah and Lawrence G. Farmer. "An Updated Measure for Assessing Subtle Rape Myths" *Social Work Research* 35, no. 2 (2011), p. 79-81.

[51] Ryan, Kathryn. p. 779.

[52] Laxer, Michael. "M is for misogyny: From frat boy chants to society" *Rabble.ca* September 9, 2013. http://rabble.ca/blogs/bloggers/michael-laxer/2013/09/m-misogyny-frat-boy-chants-to-society Accessed October 27, 2014.

[53] 20th Century Fox Television. "Movin' Out (Brian's Song)" September 30, 2007. There is some discussion as to whether the Marge Simpson scene was actually aired anywhere other than the US. This YouTube video shows the scene. https://www.youtube.com/watch?v=fA_OqFm5mWo

[54] 20th Century Fox Television. "I Dream of Jesus" *Family Guy* October 5, 2008.

[55] Bridges, AJ et al. "Aggression and sexual behavior in best-selling pornography videos: a content analysis update" *Violence Against Women* 16, no. 10 (2010).

[56] Keith, Thomas. *The Bro Code: How Contemporary Culture Creates Sexist Men* Transcript. Northampton, MA: Media Education Foundation, 2011.

[57] Foubert, John D. et al. "Pornography Viewing among Fraternity Men: Effects on Bystander Intervention, Rape Myth Acceptance and Behavioral Intent to Commit Sexual Assault" *Sexual Addiction & Compulsivity* 18, no. 4 (2011), p. 220-224.

[58] Denham, Jess. "Maroon 5 new video 'Animals' criticised for promoting sexual violence." *The Independent.* October 2, 2014. http://www.independent.co.uk/arts-entertainment/music/news/maroon-5-animals-music-video-attacked-for-promoting-sexual-violence-against-women-9770094.html Accessed October 19, 2014.

[59] Hill Catherine and Holly Kearl. *Crossing the Line: Sexual Harassment at School*

Washington: American Association of University Women, 2011, p. 6-25.
[60] Coy, Maddy et al. *"Sex without consent. I suppose that is rape." How young people in England understand sexual consent.* London: Office of the Children's Commissioner, 2013, p. 47.
[61] Ringrose, Jessica et al. *A qualitative study of children, young people and 'sexting': a report prepared for the NSPCC* London: National Society for the Prevention of Cruelty to Children, 2012, p. 7.
[62] Canadian Press. "Kamloops Sexting Case: Teens Plead Guilty to Criminal Harassment' *Huffington Post* October 28, 2014. http://www.huffingtonpost.ca/2014/10/28/kamloops-sexting-case-criminal-harassment_n_6064916.html Accessed October 29, 2014.
[63] Ringrose et al, p. 41.
[64] Ibid, p. 12.
[65] CBC News. "Amanda Todd suicide: RCMP repeatedly told of blackmailer's attempts" *CBC News* November 15, 2013 http://www.cbc.ca/news/canada/amanda-todd-suicide-rcmp-repeatedly-told-of-blackmailer-s-attempts-1.2427097 Accessed December 4, 2014.
[66] Brumfield, Ben. "7 high school players face sexual assault charges over alleged locker room hazing" *CNN* http://www.cnn.com/2014/10/11/us/new-jersey-football-abuse-scandal/index.html Accessed October 13, 2014.
[67] Hill and Kearl. p. 6-25.
[68] Collier, Katie et al. "Homophobic Name-Calling Among Secondary School Students and Its Implications for Mental Health" *Journal of Youth and Adolescence* 42, no. 3 (2013), p. 363.
[69] Gruber, James E. and Susan Fineran. "Comparing the Impact of Bullying and Sexual Harassment Victimization on the Mental and Physical Health of Adolescents" *Sex Roles* 59, no 1-2. (2008), p. 9.
[70] Funk, Leah C. and Cherie D. Werhun. "'You're Such a Girl!' The Psychological Drain of the Gender-Role Harassment of Men" *Sex Roles* 65, no. 1-2 (2011), p. 14.
[71] Collier et al, p. 365.
[72] Ringrose et al, p. 41-43.
[73] Young, Amy et al. "Adolescents' Experience of Sexual Assault by Peers: Prevalence and Nature of Victimization Occurring Within and Outside School" *Journal of Youth and Adolescence* 38, no. 8 (2009), p. 1072-1076.
[74] Davies, Michelle. "Male sexual assault victims: a selective review of the literature and implications for support services" *Aggression and Violent Behavior*, 7, no. 3 (2002), p. 206-211.
[75] Fisher, Nicola L. and Afroditi Pina. "An overview of the literature on female-perpetrated adult male sexual victimization" *Aggression and Violent Behavior*, 18, no. 1 (2013), p. 57.

[76] Davies, Michelle, p. 206.
[77] Fisher and Pina, p. 56-58.
[78] Warner Bros. Television. "Shadow" *Supernatural* February 28, 2006.
[79] Warner Bros. Television. "I'm No Angel" *Supernatural* October 22, 2013.
[80] Warner Bros. Television. "Holy Terror" *Supernatural* December 3, 2013.
[81] 20th Century Fox Television. "Dial Meg for Murder" *Family Guy* January 31, 2010.
[82] 20th Century Fox Television. "Amish Guy" *Family Guy* November 27, 2011.

Chapter Six

[1] Lerum, Kari and Shari L. Dworkin. "'Bad Girls Rule': An Interdisciplinary Feminist Commentary on the Report of the APA Task Force on the Sexualization of Girls" *Journal of Sex Research.* 46, no.4 (2009), p. 258.

[2] Boynton, Petra. "Better dicks through drugs? The penis as pharmaceutical target." *Scan: Journal of Media Arts and Culture* 1, no. 3 (2004) http://www.scan.net.au/scan/journal/display.php?journal_id=37 Accessed April 28, 2013.
[3] Examples by famous pin-up artist Gil Elvgren can be seen at http://www.thepinupfiles.com/elvgren1.html. Accessed January 20, 2015.
[4] Bordo, Susan. *The Male Body: A New Look at Men in Public and in Private.* New York: Farrar, Straus and Giroux.1999, p. 168, 180.
[5] Gill, Rosalind et al. "Body Projects and the Regulation of Normative Masculinity" *Body & Society* 11, no. 1 (2005): p.38-39.

[6] Tiggeman, Marika. "Television and Adolescent Body Image: The Role of Program Content and Viewing Motivation" *Journal of Social and Clinical Psychology.* 24, no. 3 (2005), p. 364.
[7] Moin, David. "Abercrombie & Fitch Campaign Goes Minimal, With Less Sex" *Women's Wear Daily* November 1, 2015. http://wwd.com/media-news/fashion-memopad/abercrombie-fitch-campaign-minimal-less-sex-10271917/ Accessed December 9, 2015.
[8] Gianatasio, David. "Hunkvertising: The Objectification of Men in Advertising" *Adweek* October 7, 2013. http://www.adweek.com/news/advertising-branding/hunkvertising-objectification-men-advertising-152925 Accessed February 6, 2014.
[9] An example can be seen on this Instagram page, accessed June 30, 2015: https://instagram.com/p/3KujYDJTGc/
[10] Bahadur, Nina. "Kraft Zesty Dressing Ad Offends 'One Million Moms,'

Sparks Debate. *The Huffington Post.* June 14, 2013. http://www.huffingtonpost.com/2013/06/14/kraft-zesty-dressing-ad_n_3441805.html Accessed November 20, 2013.

[11] Time Warner. *Entertainment Weekly.* #1257, May 3, 2013, p. 20-21.

[12] Gianatasio, David.

[13] Marvel Entertainment. "Marvel's Daredevil: Teaser Trailer" *YouTube* February 4, 2015. https://www.youtube.com/watch?v=XC7GPdBV9WQ Accessed February 7, 2015.

[14] Warner Bros. Pictures. "Magic Mike XXL—Official Teaser Trailer" *YouTube* February 4, 2015 https://www.youtube.com/watch?v=RwPR0q5es0A Accessed February 7, 2015.

[15] As of February, 2015 the wallpaper was available at http://wallvever.com/superman-logo-2013-wallpaper-2/.

[16] Calvin Klein. "Justin Bieber + Lara Stone—Calvin Klein Jeans Spring 2015" *YouTube* https://www.youtube.com/watch?v=K0t-aBAYym8 Accessed January 27, 2015.

[17] Ellis, Tagert. "Nick Jonas: Like a Bull in a China Shop" *Flaunt* October 21, 2014. http://flaunt.com/people/nick-jonas/ Accessed October 21, 2014.

[18] Ricciardelli, Rosemary. "Investigating Hegemonic Masculinity: Portrayals of Masculinity in Men's Lifestyle Magazines" *Sex Roles* 63, no. 1 (2010): p. 66.

[19] Lawler, Margaret and Elizabeth Nixon. "Body Dissatisfaction Among Adolescent Boys and Girls: The Effects of Body Mass, Peer Appearance Culture and Internalization of Body Ideals" *Journal of Youth and Adolescence.* 40, no. 1 (2011), p. 65.

[20] Smolak, Linda and Jonathan A. Stein. "A Longitudinal Investigation of Gender Role and Muscle Building in Adolescent Boys" *Sex Roles* 63, no. 9-10 (2010), p. 738-746.

[21] Eisenberg Marla E. et al. "Muscle-enhancing Behaviours Among Adolescent Girls and Boys" *Pediatrics* 130, no. 6 (2012), p. 1020-1021.

[22] McCalmont, Lucy. "Bryce Harper's Extreme Regimen for ESPN's Body Issue Shows Body Image is a Problem for Men Too" *The Huffington Post* July 15, 2015. http://www.huffingtonpost.com/entry/bryce-harper-body-issue-diet_55a69f57e4b04740a3deb188 Accessed July 15, 2015.

[23] Thompson, Kevin J. et al. "The Sociocultural Attitudes Towards Appearance Scale-2 (SATAQ): Development and Validation." *International Journal of Eating Disorders* 35, no. 3 (2004), p. 299.

[24] Frisen, Ann and Kristina Holmqvist. "Physical, Sociocultural, and Behavioral Factors Associated with Body-Esteem in 16-Year-Old Swedish

Boys and Girls" *Sex Roles* 63, no.5-6 (2010), p. 381.
[25] Lawler and Nixon, p. 68.
[26] Tiggeman, Marika. p. 361-381.
[27] Jones, Diana Carlson and Joy K. Crawford. "The Peer Appearance Culture During Adolescence: Gender and Body Mass Variations." *Journal of Youth and Adolescence* 35, no. 2 (2006), p. 257-269.
[28] Ricciardelli, Lina A. et al. "A Longitudinal Investigation of the Development of Weight and Muscle Concerns Among Preadolescent Boys." *Journal of Youth and Adolescence* 35, no. 2 (2006), p. 184-186.
[29] Petrie, Trent A. et al. "Biopsychosocial and Physical Correlates of Middle School Boys' and Girls' Body Satisfaction." *Sex Roles* 63, no. 9-10 (2010), p. 641-642.
[30] Lawler and Nixon, p. 68.
[31] Jones and Crawford, p. 266.
[32] Frisen and Holmqvist, p. 382.
[33] Jones and Crawford, p. 266.
[34] Field, Alison et al. "Prospective Associations of Concerns about Physique and the Development of Obesity, Binge Drinking, and Drug Use Among Adolescent Boys and Young Adult Men." *JAMA Pediatrics* 168, no. 1; (2014), p. 36-37.
[35] Gill, Rosalind et al, p. 58.
[36] Kimmel, Michael et al. (eds). *Cultural Encyclopedia of the Penis*. Lanham, MD: Rowman & Littlefield, 2014, p. 1.
[37] Boynton, Petra.
[38] Anonymous. *The Romance of Lust*. Kindle Edition.
[39] Zilbergeld, Bernard as quoted in McKee, Alan. "Does size matter? Dominant discourses about penises in Western Culture." *Cultural Studies Review* 10, no. 2: (2004), p. 178.
[40] Maddison, Stephen. "The Biopolitics of the Penis" *Cultural Studies Now* Conference, 2007. http://culturalstudiesresearch.org/wp-content/uploads/2012/10/MaddisonBiopoliticsPenis.pdf Accessed February 17, 2014.
[41] Löfgren-Mårtenson, Lotta and Sven-Axel Månsson. "Lust, Love, and Life: A Qualitative Study of Swedish Adolescents' Perceptions and Experiences with Pornography" *Journal of Sex Research*. 47, no. 6 (2010): p. 7.
[42] Kimmel et al. p. 2.
[43] Lever, Janet et al. "Does Size Matter? Men's and Women's Views on Penis Size Across the Lifespan" *Psychology of Men & Masculinity* 7, no. 3 (2006), p. 129.
[44] Shamloul, Rany. "Treatment of Men Complaining of Short Penis" *Urology* 65, no. 6 (2005), p. 1184.
[45] Lever et al, p. 134.

[46] Morrison, T.G. et al. "Correlates of genital perceptions among Canadian post-secondary students." *Electronic Journal of Human Sexuality*. 8 (2005).
[47] Lever et al.
[48] Flo Rida. *GDFR* Rap Genius. http://genius.com/4809131/Flo-rida-gdfr-goin-down-for-real/So-that-birthday-cake-get-the-cobra Accessed February 27, 2015.
[49] T.I. *No Mediocre* Rap Genius http://genius.com/3327762/Ti-no-mediocre/What-she-say-when-she-got-to-sit Accessed February 27, 2015.
[50] Thicke, Robin "Blurred Lines" *Vevo* http://www.vevo.com/watch/robin-thicke/Blurred-Lines-(Unrated-Version)/USUV71300526 Accessed March 30, 2013.
[51] Boynton, p. 1.
[52] Attwood, 2005, p. 92.
[53] Comite, Florence. *Keep It Up*. http://www.keepitupbook.com/keepitupbook/index?keycode=240597 Accessed February 7, 2015.
[54] The word "misfire" was used in an article on Men't Fitness to indicate that a man climaxed too soon. Madison, Amber. "Ask Men's Fitness: How Long Do Women Really Want to Have Sex?" *Men's Fitness* February 8, 2015. http://www.mensfitness.com/women/sex-tips/ask-mens-fitness-how-long-do-women-really-want-have-sex Accessed February 17, 2015.
[55] Westwood, Michael and Jorge Pinzon. "Adolescent male health." *Paediatric Child Health* 13, no. 1 (2008), p. 32.
[56] Shamloul, p. 1184.
[57] Wylie, Kevan R. and Ian Eardley. "Penile size and the 'small penis syndrome.'" *BJUI* 99, no. 6 (2007), p. 1451.
[58] Smith, Marshall. "Youth Viewing Sexually Explicit Material Online: Addressing the Elephant on the Screen" *Sexuality Research and Social Policy*. 10, no.1 (2013): p. 65, 72.
[59] Pappas, Stephanie. "Size Doesn't Matter: 'Penis Shame' Is All in Guys' Heads" *LiveScience* October 4, 2013. http://www.livescience.com/40192-penis-shame-guys-heads.html Accessed February 17, 2015.

Chapter Seven

[1] Fisher, Deborah A. et al "Televised sexual content and parental mediation: Influences on adolescent sexuality" *Media Psychology* 12, no. 2 (2009): p. 122.

[2] Gill, Rosalind. "Media, Empowerment and the 'Sexualization of Culture' Debates" *Sex Roles* 66, no. 11-12 (2012): p. 739.
[3] Huang, David Y. C. "Parental Monitoring During Early Adolescence Deters Adolescent Sexual Initiation: Discrete-Time Survival Mixture

Analysis" *Journal of Child and Family Studies.* 20, no. 4. (2011) p. 511-520.
[4] Price, Myeshia N. and Janet Shibley Hyde. "When Two Isn't Better Than One: Predictors of Early Sexual Activity in Adolescence Using a Cumulative Risk Model" *Journal of Youth and Adolescence.* 38, no. 8 (2009): p. 1061-1062.
[5] Fisher, 122.
[6] Brown, Lyn Mikel et al. *Packaging Boyhood: Saving our Sons from Superheroes, Slackers, and Other Media Stereotypes.* New York: St. Martin's Press, 2009. p. 267.
[7] Fisher et al, p. 133-35.
[8] Day, Lori and Charlotte Kugler. *Her Next Chapter: How Mother-Daughter Book Clubs Can Help Girls Navigate Malicious Media, Risky Relationships, Girl Gossip, and So Much More.* Chicago: Chicago Review Press, 2014, p. 47.
[9] Wardy, Melissa Atkins. *Redefining Girly: How Parents Can Fight the Stereotyping and Sexualizing of Girlhood, From Birth to Tween.* Chicago: Chicago Review Press, 2014, p. 103.
[10] Huang, David Y. C. "Parental Monitoring During Early Adolescence Deters Adolescent Sexual Initiation: Discrete-Time Survival Mixture Analysis" *Journal of Child and Family Studies.* 20, no. 4. (2011) p. 511-520.
[11] Maxwell, Kimberly A. "Friends: The Role of Peer Influence Across Adolescent Risk Behaviors" *Journal of Youth and Adolescence.* 31, no. 4 (2002): p. 267-277.
[12] Smith, Marshall, p. 73.
[13] Smith, p. 73.
[14] Canadian Centre for Child Protection. *Be Smart, Strong & Safe.* http://www.smartstrongsafe.ca/pdfs/SmartStrongSafe_ActivityBooklet_en.pdf Winnipeg: Kids in the Know.
[15] Flood, Michael. "The Harms of Pornography Exposure Among Children and Young People." *Child Abuse Review* 18, no. 6 (2009), p. 393.
[16] Weber, Mathias et al. "Peers, Parents and Pornography: Exploring Adolescents' Exposure to Sexually Explicit Material and Its Developmental Correlates" *Sexuality & Culture* 16, no. 4 (2012), p. 409-10.
[17] Forsberg, Manne. *Sex for Guys: A Groundwork Guide.* Toronto: Groundwood Books, 2007, p. 96-97.
[18] Peter and Valkenburg, 2010, p. 393.
[19] Smith, Marshall. "Youth Viewing Sexually Explicit Material Online: Addressing the Elephant on the Screen" *Sexuality Research and Social Policy.* 10, no.1 (2013): p. 73-74.
[20] Shewmaker, Jen. "Teaching Kids About Consent: Yes means yes" *jennifershewmaker.com* September 29, 2014. http://jennifershewmaker.com/2014/09/29/teaching-kids-about-consent-yes-means-yes/ Accessed October 1, 2014.

21 Jhally, Sut. *Asking For It: The Ethics & Erotics of Sexual Consent*. Transcript. Media Education Foundation. 2010.
22 Talbot, Michael. "CityNews' Shauna Hunt confronts men about 'FHRITP' vulgarities" *680 News* May 11, 2015. http://www.680news.com/2015/05/11/citynews-shauna-hunt-confronts-men-fhritp-vulgarities/ Accessed June 8, 2015.
23 CBC reporter Shannon Martin talked about how the FHRITP phrase affected her in an interview that would be very instructive for boys. http://www.cbc.ca/player/AudioMobile/Metro%2BMorning/ID/2667112599/
24 Keith, Thomas. *The Bro Code: How Contemporary Culture Creates Sexist Men* Transcript. Northampton, MA: Media Education Foundation, 2011.
25 McMahon, Sarah and Lawrence G. Farmer. "An Updated Measure for Assessing Subtle Rape Myths" *Social Work Research* 35, no. 2 (2011), p. 79-81.
26 Gruber, James E. and Susan Fineran. "Comparing the Impact of Bullying and Sexual Harassment Victimization on the Mental and Physical Health of Adolescents" *Sex Roles* 59, no 1-2. (2008), p. 1-13.
27 Davies, Michelle. "Male sexual assault victims: a selective review of the literature and implications for support services" *Aggression and Violent Behavior*, 7, no. 3 (2002), p. 205.

28 Botta, Renée. "For Your Health? The Relationship Between Magazine Reading and Adolescents' Body Image and Eating Disturbances" *Sex Roles* 48, no. 9/10 (2003), p. 389-399.
29 Hatoum, Ida Jodette and Deborah Belle. "Mags and Abs: Media Consumption and Bodily Concerns in Men" *Sex Roles* 51, no. 7/8 (2004), p. 391-407.
30 Alexander, Susan M. "Stylish Hard Bodies: Branded Masculinity in *Men's Health* Magazine." *Sociological Perspectives* 46, no.4 (2003), p. 535-554.
31 Pope, Harrison G. et al. *The Adonis Complex: How to Identify, Treat, and Prevent Body Obsession in Men and Boys*. New York: Touchstone, 2000, p. 174.
32 Westwood, Michael and Jorge Pinzon. "Adolescent male health." *Paediatric Child Health* 13, no. 1 (2008), p. 32.
33 Madaras, Lynda. *The "What's Happening to My Body?" Book for Boys*. New York: HarperCollins, 2007, p. 53.
34 Male Edge. "Natural Penis Enlargement" http://www.maleedge.com/en/ Accessed June 12. 2015.
35 Oderda, Marco and Paolo Gontero. "Non-invasive methods of penile lengthening: fact or fiction?" *BJU International* 107, no. 8 (2011), p. 1278-1282.
36 Wardy, p. 173.

www.ingramcontent.com/pod-product-compliance
Lightning Source LLC
Chambersburg PA
CBHW071458040426
42444CB00008B/1403